Human Trafficking

Other Books in the Global Viewpoints Series

Human Trafficking

Lita Sorensen, Book Editor

Published in 2020 by Greenhaven Publishing, LLC
353 3rd Avenue, Suite 255, New York, NY 10010

Copyright © 2020 by Greenhaven Publishing, LLC

First Edition

Articles in Greenhaven Publishing anthologies are often edited for length to meet page
requirements. In addition, original titles of these works are changed to clearly present
the main thesis and to explicitly indicate the author's opinion. Every effort is made to
ensure that Greenhaven Publishing accurately reflects the original intent of the authors.
Every effort has been made to trace the owners of the copyrighted material.

Cover image: NurPhoto/Getty Images, © Can Stock Photo/
Volokhatiuk (clouds), © Tsiumpa/Dreamstime.com (earth)

Map: frees/Shutterstock.com

Library of Congress Cataloging-in-Publication Data

Names: Sorensen, Lita, editor.
Title: Human trafficking / Lita Sorensen, book editor.
Description: First edition. | New York, NY : Greenhaven Publishing, 2020. | Series: Global
viewpoints | Includes bibliographical references and index. | Audience: Grades 9–12.
Identifiers: LCCN 2019022620 | ISBN 9781534506503 (library
binding) | ISBN 9781534506497 (paperback)
Subjects: LCSH: Human trafficking—Juvenile literature. | Human
trafficking—Prevention—Juvenile literature.
Classification: LCC HQ281 .H8323 2020 | DDC 364.15/51—dc23
LC record available at https://lccn.loc.gov/2019022620

Manufactured in the United States of America

Website: http://greenhavenpublishing.com

Contents

Chapter 2: Causes and Effects of Human Trafficking

Chapter 3: Types of Human Trafficking and Its Global Impact

From Nigeria to Catania, Italy, a lurid tale of voodoo, deceit, and abuse, preying on the innocence of underage girls.

Chapter 4: Putting a Stop to Human Trafficking

Foreword

*"The problems of all of humanity can
only be solved by all of humanity."*
—Swiss author Friedrich Dürrenmatt

Global interdependence has become an undeniable reality. Mass media and technology have increased worldwide access to information and created a society of global citizens. Understanding and navigating this global community is a challenge, requiring a high degree of information literacy and a new level of learning sophistication.

Building on the success of its flagship series, Opposing Viewpoints, Greenhaven Publishing has created the Global Viewpoints series to examine a broad range of current, often controversial topics of worldwide importance from a variety of international perspectives. Providing students and other readers with the information they need to explore global connections and think critically about worldwide implications, each Global Viewpoints volume offers a panoramic view of a topic of widespread significance.

Drugs, famine, immigration—a broad, international treatment is essential to do justice to social, environmental, health, and political issues such as these. Junior high, high school, and early college students, as well as general readers, can all use Global Viewpoints anthologies to discern the complexities relating to each issue. Readers will be able to examine unique national perspectives while, at the same time, appreciating the interconnectedness that global priorities bring to all nations and cultures.

Material in each volume is selected from a diverse range of sources, including journals, magazines, newspapers, nonfiction books, speeches, government documents, pamphlets, organization newsletters, and position papers. Global Viewpoints is truly global, with material drawn primarily from international sources available in English and secondarily from US sources with extensive international coverage.

Features of each volume in the Global Viewpoints series include:

- An **annotated table of contents** that provides a brief summary of each essay in the volume, including the name of the country or area covered in the essay.

- An **introduction** specific to the volume topic.

- A world map to help readers locate the countries or areas covered in the essays.

- For each viewpoint, **an introduction** that contains notes about the author and source of the viewpoint explains why material from the specific country is being presented, summarizes the main points of the viewpoint, and offers three **guided reading questions** to aid in understanding and comprehension.

- **For further discussion** questions that promote critical thinking by asking the reader to compare and contrast aspects of the viewpoints or draw conclusions about perspectives and arguments.

- A worldwide list of **organizations to contact** for readers seeking additional information.

- A **periodical bibliography** for each chapter and a **bibliography of books** on the volume topic to aid in further research.

- A comprehensive **subject index** to offer access to people, places, events, and subjects cited in the text.

Global Viewpoints is designed for a broad spectrum of readers who want to learn more about current events, history, political science, government, international relations, economics, environmental science, world cultures, and sociology—students doing research for class assignments or debates, teachers and faculty seeking to supplement course materials, and others wanting to understand current issues better. By presenting how people in various countries perceive the root causes, current consequences, and proposed solutions to worldwide challenges, Global Viewpoints volumes offer readers opportunities to enhance their global awareness and their knowledge of cultures worldwide.

Introduction

*"Imagine having all of your freedoms
taken away, being forced to work
against your will, and constantly
living under the threat of violence—
in short, being forced to live as a
slave. Sadly, this situation is a reality
for millions of children, women, and
men each year as part of the global
human trafficking industry."*
—Rep. Bill Flores, *Waco Tribune Herald*, May 18, 2014

Some say that human slavery never actually went away, despite being outlawed by nearly all developed nations more than a century ago. This is the mostly hidden world of human trafficking, or the sale or coercion of human beings into prostitution or forced labor, child sexual exploitation, illegal adoptions, involuntary marriage, and illicit organ sales. According to the Polaris Project, a nonprofit, non-governmental organization dedicated to combatting and preventing modern-day slavery and human trafficking, trafficking in human beings is a multi-billion-dollar criminal enterprise that violates the human rights and freedoms of an estimated 24.9 million people globally.

In some estimations, the problem is not going away and instead has only gained traction, growing exponentially in most countries around the world, with developed nations serving as host countries and economically struggling countries serving as targeted sources for the victims of exploitation in many instances.

Global Viewpoints: Human Trafficking contains a selection of viewpoints intended to clarify the issues surrounding human trafficking around the world, including the fact that this problem seems to affect all cultures, despite international inroads made into acknowledgement of fundamental freedoms, human rights, and their abuses in the last couple centuries. Chapter One provides an overview of the worldwide problem, with authors contributing varying outlooks, including a piece on the proper use of terminology associated with human trafficking, types of human trafficking and their specific complications, including child sexual exploitation.

Chapter Two delves into the plights of victims and the causes and effects of human trafficking, offering viewpoints ranging from a look at the vulnerable groups prone to being exploited by traffickers, pieces from the point of view of victims, a look at bonded labor and other forms of modern-day slavery, and a piece on how technology has aided the spread of human trafficking all over the world.

Chapter Three takes a deeper look into the various types of human trafficking and the impact it has around the globe. Viewpoints explored include an in-depth examination of sexual trafficking, where the coercion and deception used to exploit victims is particularly virulent, a piece on the illegal adoption trade, and an article on the trafficking of human organs, which most often is coerced and surreptitious. The chapter also covers forced marriage with a mention of the American FLDS church, which has been accused of coercing underage girls into unwanted and illegal marriages, and includes a story highlighting the unique narratives of various victims of human trafficking.

Chapter Four focuses on current measures being taken to combat human trafficking crimes, human trafficking laws and policies that are already in place and new international developments, a piece on how technology is being used to combat trafficking in persons, a viewpoint of human trafficking and sexual exploitation from the perspective of law enforcement, where it has been found that drug traffickers are often human traffickers, too, and viewpoints on what services and social safety nets are now in place to aid the survivors of trafficking once they return to normal life.

Human trafficking is a crime that can be described simply as the stealing of human freedom and dignity for illicit personal profit. Whether defined as a modern-day form of slavery or another, related form of exploitation and manipulation, it has been with us for hundreds of years and has affected—and continues to affect— millions of people the world over. It is an important, often hidden issue that needs to be examined in a multifaceted way in order to be fully understood and brought out of the shadows where it thrives. The survey of viewpoints that follows provides a context with that goal in mind.

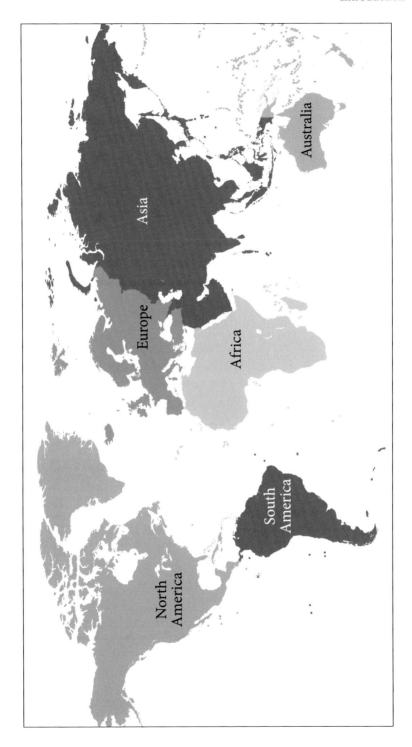

CHAPTER 1

Human Trafficking Around the World

In the United States, Reconsidering the Use of the Term "Modern Day Slavery" for Human Trafficking

Sarah Harrison

In the following viewpoint, Megan Thomas argues that there should be a clarification of terms when we are speaking and writing about human trafficking as opposed to historical slavery in America, which has always been based on race. Sarah Harrison is an Anti-Human Trafficking Specialist at the North Carolina Coalition Against Sexual Assault, an inclusive, statewide alliance working to end sexual violence through education, advocacy, and legislation. She provides training and technical assistance to pilot sites statewide and works with community partners to combat human trafficking in North Carolina.

As you read, consider the following questions:

1. What is the author advocating regarding the use of terminology when talking about human trafficking?
2. What is the reasoning behind the author taking this stance?
3. How might this be classified as a particularly "American" viewpoint?

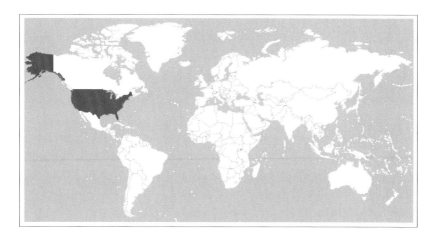

When you start searching the internet for information regarding human trafficking, it is likely that within a few clicks you will run across the term "modern day slavery." This term has been used by everyone from local non-profits to law enforcement task forces to President Obama, and it has largely been accepted and solidified as a holistic descriptor of what human trafficking is.

However, it is important for us as a movement to take a moment to reflect on why this term, and particularly the use of the word "slavery," may intend to be helpful in relaying impact but in fact is exploitative.

We must hold ourselves to a standard that centers our collective humanity, and not advance our personal/organizational/movement "success" at the expense of harming communities who've experienced (and continue to experience) oppression and marginalization. What I am commenting on below is specific to the American context of the word slavery. The history of this country's use of the term and institution of slavery is unique and must be considered.

1. Historical Slavery Never Ended

Historical slavery, or the state-sanctioned control of brown and black bodies, has never really ended; it has just molded and changed to fit the times. When looking at the 13th amendment, which was passed in 1865, there are significant loopholes which were intentionally created to ensure there would remain a "free work force." (For more information on this, check out Ava DuVernay's documentary *13th* on Netflix now.) From Jim Crow-era laws through to today, that free work force looks like those who are incarcerated through the criminal (in)justice system, which impacts people of color at astronomically higher rates. To say "modern day slavery" is to ignore the continuation of historical slavery into this century and through today.

2. Historical Slavery Was Legal; Human Trafficking Is Not

The nineteenth-century slave trade was protected by law, and it utilized fugitive slave laws, slave patrols, and the courts to promote and maintain the institution. Now however, slavery is not protected by law. Author of *Life Interrupted: Trafficking in Forced Labor in the United States*, Denise Brennan, argues that human trafficking "is not the law of the land. It is not protected by a legal framework that is based on race, and no one is born into a race-based enslaved status."

3. There Is Nothing Modern About This Form of Exploitation

If we continue thinking in the American context, we can look as far back as the early 1600s, when colonization started taking place and Native American people were systematically harmed to obtain control of the land. The bodies and lives of Native women were seen as lesser than and something to be used for personal pleasure or financial gain. This existed back then and has continued today. Our government does not even track the number of Native women who go missing annually. There is no clearer sign that a government does not care for a person's body than if it is not even willing to notice when it goes missing.

4. Slavery (in This American Context) Is Based on Race; Exploitation Is Based in Rape Culture and Socially Constructed Risk Factors

Enslavement in America is baked into the very creation of race and the black and brown bodies who built this country and made the economy as "successful" as it is. Sexual exploitation, which certainly wages war against bodies, is grounded in a complex foundation of rape culture, race, and socially constructed risk factors (food/housing insecurity, sexist culture/household, unrepresentative leadership, etc.) that make people more likely to either cause harm or to be a victim. The demonization of black and brown bodies that historical slavery is founded on was manifested to enable slavery to continue. We see examples of this when we look at cases like John Punch or Bacon's Rebellion. If these names or events don't sound familiar to you, they are worth a quick search!

5. Using Terms for Shock Value

The term "modern day slavery" gained popularity within the last 25 years and is most often used to elicit shock from those reading. I understand the need to engage community partners and convince them that this work is important, but to mobilize the history of slavery without really analyzing or exploring what that was and the current ramifications of this history is exploitative. When this term is activated, it's often using the emotional power that's attached to historical slavery without actually being connected to it. It is our job as advocates to consider and create ways of reaching out and creating spaces for education and understanding of the issue, without causing more harm.

6. There Isn't Consistency

From a completely practical standpoint, there isn't an established definition of what we mean when using the term "modern day slavery." Are we combining all forms of forced labor and sexual exploitation? Does this include child marriage or debt bondage?

When working on prevention, it's crucial to know what we are trying to prevent, as that will shape everything from who the target audience is, to implementation tactics, to whose voices need to be included in the planning conversation.

I understand if these points alone don't feel convincing enough to stop using the term "modern day slavery." And certainly when a survivor identifies a word to describe their experience, that should always be honored and supported. I do however hope you have taken a moment of pause for self-reflection as an individual or organization and asked—why do I/we use this language? Who is it benefitting? And more importantly, who is it harming?

VIEWPOINT 2

There Are Many Types of Human Trafficking

Office of the United Nations High Commissioner for Human Rights

In the following viewpoint the United Nations provides an overview of international efforts to address and define human trafficking, which can take many exploitive forms. It also gives context for the relationship between universal human rights violations and trafficking in persons, recognizing that certain groups should be given special consideration and protection due to their vulnerability. The Office of the United Nations High Commissioner for Human Rights, established in 1993, is a department of the Secretariat of the United Nations working to promote and protect the human rights that are guaranteed under international law and stipulated in the Universal Declaration of Human Rights document formulated in 1948.

As you read, consider the following questions:

1. How is human trafficking defined by international law, and what are the different types of "trafficking in persons?"
2. What are ways in which violations of human rights and human trafficking overlap?
3. Which vulnerable groups are often targeted for trafficking and what are the reasons for this?

Human trafficking usually refers to the process through which individuals are placed or maintained in an exploitative situation for economic gain. International efforts to address it can be traced back to the nineteenth century. However, it is only over the past two decades that a comprehensive legal framework has developed around the issue. The adoption of the Protocol to Prevent, Suppress and Punish the Trafficking in Persons, especially women and children, supplementing the United Nations Convention against Transnational Organized Crime in 2000 was a milestone that provided the first internationally agreed definition of "trafficking in persons": "the recruitment, transportation, transfer, harbouring or receipt of persons, by means of the threat or use of force or other forms of coercion, of abduction, of fraud, of deception, of the abuse of power or of a position of vulnerability or of the giving or receiving of payments or benefits to achieve the consent of a person having control over another person, for the purpose of exploitation. Exploitation shall include, at a minimum, the exploitation of the prostitution of others or other forms of sexual exploitation, forced labour or services, slavery or practices similar to slavery, servitude or the removal of organs."

Despite the existence of a comprehensive international legal framework, millions of children, women and men continue to be trafficked each year, in all regions and in most countries of the world. Victims may be trafficked within a country or across a border for various purposes, including forced and exploitative labour in factories, farms and private households, sexual exploitation, forced marriage and organ removal. The clandestine nature of trafficking makes it difficult to quantify the phenomenon. According to the Walk Free Foundation and ILO Global Estimates (https://www.alliance87.org/2017ge/), 25 million people were subjected to forced labour and sexual exploitation in 2016 worldwide. UNODC's 2016 Global Report (http://www.unodc.org/documents/data-and-analysis/glotip/2016_Global_Report_on_Trafficking_in_Persons.pdf) on identified victims shows that 51% of victims are women, 21% men, 20% girls and 8% boys. Among those victims, 45% have

---

Combatting Human Trafficking

Human trafficking affects virtually all OSCE (Organization for Security and Cooperation in Europe) states, either as countries of origin or destination. This modern form of slavery is an affront to human dignity, often involving psychological terror and physical violence. Human trafficking engages issues of human rights and rule of law, of law enforcement and crime control, of inequality and discrimination, of corruption, economic deprivation and migration.

As such, human trafficking affects virtually all OSCE participating States as countries of origin, transit or destination. This modern form of slavery is an affront to human dignity, often involving psychological terror and physical violence. The OSCE addresses many issues relevant to human trafficking: human rights and rule of law; corruption and crime control; discrimination and inequality; economic, labour, and migration policies.

In 2003, the Organization set up the Office and post of Special Representative and Co-ordinator for Combating Trafficking in Human Beings to help participating States develop and implement effective policies for combating human trafficking. The Office of the Special Representative promotes a victim-centred and human rights-based approach in protecting victims.

The OSCE Action Plan to Combat Trafficking in Human Beings provides the framework for OSCE activities in support of the anti-trafficking efforts

---

been trafficked for sexual exploitation and 38% for forced labour. In recent years, trafficking has also thrived amongst populations living in or fleeing conflict situations.

Even though our knowledge on trafficking in persons remains incomplete, it is widely acknowledged that certain factors make an individual, a social group or a community more vulnerable to trafficking and related exploitation. Discrimination in the denial of economic and social rights are critical factors in rendering certain persons more vulnerable than others. Discrimination and poverty results in fewer and poorer life choices, and may lead certain individuals to take risks and make decisions that they would never have done if their basic needs were being met. This of OSCE participating States. It contains core recommendations for action at the national level, known as the "3 Ps":

- Prevention, including awareness-raising and addressing root causes;
- Prosecution, including investigation and co-operation with international law enforcement; and
- Protection of victims' rights, including assistance and compensation.

In 2013, the OSCE added a fourth "P"—a chapter on partnerships—highlighting the need for enhanced co-operation with international organizations and other partners, including on issues related to law enforcement, National Referral Mechanisms (NRMs) and joint work between public institutions and the private sector.

A number of OSCE field operations help strengthen the capacity of national and local authorities, as well as civil society organizations, in preventing and fighting human trafficking, strengthening prosecution and assisting victims. They run seminars and training courses for, among others, police, border-guards, judges, prosecutors, lawyers, social workers, religious leaders, the media; surveys and studies; and information campaigns for the public.

"Combating Human Trafficking," OSCE

lack of genuine choice can in turn increase the vulnerability of certain groups, such as minorities, migrants and women and girls, to trafficking. In addition to economic deprivation and inequalities, gender and race-based discrimination are important factors that may limit life choices and make some persons and communities more vulnerable to trafficking.

The links between human rights and trafficking in persons are manifold. Human rights are universal and hence victims of trafficking are entitled to the full range of human rights, irrespective of their sex, age, race, ethnic origin, nationality, migratory status or other distinction. International human rights law also recognizes that certain groups, such as women and children, require additional or special protection. Different human rights are relevant at different points in the trafficking cycle. Some are especially relevant to the causes of trafficking. This is when a violation of human rights, for instance the violation of the right to an adequate standard of living, lead to increase vulnerability of a person. Other human rights are relevant to the actual process of trafficking. In fact, trafficking and associated practices such as slavery, sexual exploitation, child labour, forced labour, debt bondage and forced marriage, are themselves violations of basic human rights and are prohibited under international human rights law. Finally, certain human rights concern the response to trafficking, such as the right to access to justice, the right to effective remedies, and the right to a fair trial.

While the link between human rights and human trafficking is rather clear, it does not necessarily follow that human rights will be at the centre of responses to trafficking. The human rights-based approach places the victim at the centre of any effective and credible action. It also extends the focus to the root causes that underlie trafficking, maintain impunity for traffickers, and deny justice to victims, such as patterns of discrimination, unjust distribution of power, demand for goods and services derived from exploitation, and complicity of the public sector. The human rights based approach also acknowledges that governments are responsible for protecting and promoting the rights of all persons within their jurisdiction, including non-citizens, and therefore have a legal obligation to work towards eliminating trafficking and related exploitation.

The UN Human Rights Office is at the forefront of efforts to promote a human rights-based approach to trafficking in persons. The Office has developed Recommended Principles and Guidelines on Human Rights and Human Trafficking (https://www.ohchr.org/Documents/Publications/Traffickingen.pdf) and its extensive Commentary (https://www.ohchr.org/Documents/Publications/Commentary_Human_Trafficking_en.pdf) that aim to help all those involved in anti-trafficking efforts to fully integrate human rights into their analysis and responses to trafficking. The document includes seventeen recommended principles that address the following core areas: (a) the primacy of human rights; (b) preventing trafficking; (c) protection and assistance; (d) criminalization, punishment and redress. Additionally, eleven recommended guidelines provide practical measures for their implementation.

Human Trafficking Is Fueled by Poverty and the Promise of Profits

Sarah Ferguson

A combination of factors fuels human trafficking, or the buying and selling of people, according to the following viewpoint, written by Sarah Ferguson of UNICEF (The United Nations Children's Fund). Main drivers include the promise of high profits with very little risk or chances of perpetrators being prosecuted. Unstable regional conditions and poverty also promote victimhood, with traffickers exploiting those left vulnerable under these sorts of conditions. Sarah Ferguson is Editorial Consultant for UNICEF USA, a branch of the United Nations that works to provide emergency food and healthcare and other assistance to children and mothers in countries around the world.

As you read, consider the following questions:

1. How do poverty and unstable conditions help to create situations where human trafficking is prevalent?
2. What are systemic inequalities?
3. How does the author relate human trafficking to modern-day slavery?

At its most basic form, human trafficking is the buying and selling of people. It exists across continents and is facilitated

"What Fuels Human Trafficking?" by Sarah Ferguson, Courtesy of UNICEF USA, January 13, 2017, Reprinted by permission.

through a variety of venues, but ultimately—human trafficking is an industry, and it profits from the exploitation of people.

Human trafficking has been likened to modern-day slavery, and in many respects, the similarities are obvious.

It's the 21st century and children, women, and men are still being forced to work in inhumane conditions, for long hours, for little to no pay.

Slavery of the past was an accepted economic practice, but today, human trafficking is a criminal activity. Slavery used to systematically exploit specific groups of people, while today, anyone can be a human trafficking victim regardless of ethnicity, nationality, gender, age, or economic status. Human trafficking is now facilitated online and through social media. Traffickers use love and affection as control mechanisms, and those victimized might not even self-identify as victims. Human trafficking is an incredibly complex issue based on dozens of contributing factors. To understand how trafficking exists today, what it looks like, and why it is sustained, we are going to explore three factors that give it fuel.

1. High reward-low risk
2. Supply and demand
3. Systemic inequalities

First, human trafficking is fueled by a high reward, low risk dynamic. This means that traffickers can expect to make a lot of money with minimal fear of punishment or legal consequence. It's the second most profitable illegal industry—second only to the drug trade. And while drugs are sold in one transaction, human beings can be sold over and over again. The costs are low and the profits are extremely high. The International Labour Organization estimates that profits from human trafficking and forced labor are $150 billion annually.

But what are the risks?

The table below shows the Global Enforcement Data from the 2015 Trafficking in Persons Report. It describes the estimated amount of human trafficking prosecutions and convictions around the world each year.

Global Enforcement Data, 2015

Year	Prosecutions	Convictions	Victims Identified	New/Amended Legislation
2007	5,682 (490)	3,427 (326)		28
2008	5,212 (312)	2,983 (104)	30,961	26
2009	5,606 (432)	4,166 (335)	49,105	33
2010	6,017 (607)	3,619 (237)	33,113	17
2011	7,909 (456)	3,969 (278)	42,291 (15,205)	15
2012	7,705 (1,153)	4,746 (518)	44,570 (17,368)	21
2013	9,460 (1,199)	5,776 (470)	44,758 (10,603)	58
2014	10,051 (418)	4,443 (216)	44,462 (11,438)	20

The number of prosecutions is shockingly low for an industry that victimizes an estimated 21 million people around the world. Lasting legal consequences for human traffickers are still minimal and rare. Traffickers know they can sell and exploit others and little will be done to stop them.

Second, human trafficking is fueled by the economic principles of supply and demand.

Human trafficking is the only industry in which the supply and demand are the same thing: human beings. People demanding the sale of people.

High demand drives the high volume of supply. Increasing demand from consumers for cheap goods incentivizes corporations to demand cheap labor, often forcing those at the bottom of the supply chain to exploit workers. Secondly, increased demand for commercial sex—especially with young girls and boys—incentivizes commercial sex venues including strip clubs, pornography, and prostitution to recruit and exploit children.

Lastly, systemic inequalities and disparities make certain groups much more vulnerable to exploitation. Mass displacement, conflict, extreme poverty, lack of access to education and job opportunities, violence, and harmful social norms like child marriage are all factors that push individuals into situations of trafficking. Families living in extreme poverty or families in situations of desperation are more likely to accept risky job offers. When girls aren't allowed to learn, parents are more likely to sell their daughters to men for marriage.

Ultimately, harmful social norms and systemic inequity fuel trafficking because traffickers target vulnerability. Traffickers look for people living in poverty, those who are desperate, those without legitimate job options, those without educational opportunities, and the ones looking for a way to escape violence.

If we never address these basic human rights violations, we will never see the day when trafficking no longer exists.

Want to take action? You can address the three factors that fuel trafficking by taking the following three steps.

1. Advocate for legislation that increases penalties for traffickers and enhances protections for victims.

2. Learn how your buying habits contribute to the demand for exploitative labor by going to Slaveryfootprint.org. Then take steps to make ethical purchases by shopping for Fair Trade products. Fair Trade certification ensures that no child or slave labor contributed to the making of a product.

3. Support UNICEF's development work to lessen vulnerabilities for children around the world here: https://donate.unicefusa.org/page/contribute/ donate-to-central-african-republic-16207?utm_ campaign=20190306_Emergencies&utm_ medium=TV&utm_source=NBC&utm_content=CAR_ Ad&ms=TV_DIG_2019_Emergencies_20190306_ NBC_CAR_Ad_none_none&initialms=TV_DIG_2019_ Emergencies_20190306_NBC_CAR_Ad_none_none

The End Trafficking project is an awareness-based initiative to educate communities on the issue of human trafficking and mobilize them to take action. If you would like to support the End

Trafficking project, you can host a fundraiser or film screening by filling out our application here: https://www.unicefusa. org/supporters/volunteers/fundraisers or download our free educational resources here: https://www.unicefusa.org/mission/ protect/trafficking/end/resources.

In Latin America, the Middle East, North America, the Pacific, Asia, and Africa, Children Are Exploited in Sexual Tourism

Angela Hawke and Alison Raphael

In the following excerpted viewpoint, Angela Hawke and Alison Raphael offer an executive summary of their larger report on child sexual exploitation across the globe, with each continental region explored individually for issues specific to that part of the world. Key findings and conclusions regarding recommendations to combat the growing problem, including the cooperation of service organizations and law enforcement bodies, and the need for further studies are presented. Angela Hawke was Deputy Media Chief for UNICEF worldwide and former Senior Editor and Writer at the Overseas Development Institute. Alison Raphael works as a consultant for UNICEF and a writer for ECPAT International.

"Global Study on Sexual Exploitation of Children in Travel and Tourism 2016," by Angela Hawke and Alison Raphael, World Tourism Organization. Reprinted by permission.

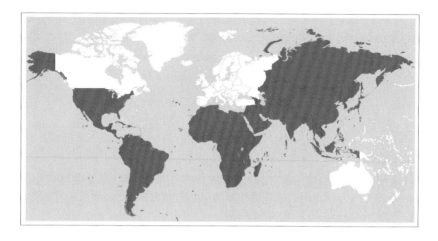

As you read, consider the following questions:

1. How do modern technology and interconnectedness help to spread the occurrence of child sexual exploitation in sexual tourism throughout the world?
2. How does wealth and/or poverty influence global child sexual tourism?
3. What key conclusions do the authors make to help combat global sexual tourism and the exploitation of child victims?

D espite 20 years of efforts, the sexual exploitation of children in travel and tourism (SECTT) has expanded across the globe and out-paced every attempt to respond at the international and national level. The results of the first comprehensive global study on SECTT confirm that no region is untouched by this crime and no country is "immune." In an increasingly interconnected world, more people are on the move and even the most remote parts of the planet are now within reach, thanks to cheaper travel and the spread of the Internet. As a result, the risks of child sexual exploitation are increasing.

The impact on each individual child cannot be over-stated. For survivors, the legacy can include severe and life-long physical, emotional and psychological damage. As well as consuming its child victims, SECTT also fractures families and local cultures, and undermines the future prospects of entire communities. On the one hand, inaction on this crime can have serious social and economic consequences. On the other hand, effective action must be informed by hard evidence.

SECTT is, by its very nature, secretive and hidden. Little is known about what is happening and where, about the victims and perpetrators, and, very importantly, about what actually works to stop the abuse. To date, the lack of solid information about this crime, coupled with silence or even tolerance, has kept SECTT far too low on the policy agenda.

The Global Study on SECTT aims to bring this gross violation of children's rights into the light, and marks the 20th anniversary of the 1st World Congress on the Sexual Exploitation of Children. Guided by a High-Level Taskforce and informed by detailed studies from every region and many countries, as well as contributions from experts and children, the Global Study is the first (and, to date, the only) research initiative on SECTT to explore emerging trends and possible solutions.

Key Findings by Region

A range of findings have emerged from the nine regional reports carried out for the global study. The reports revealed some similarities, such as increasing diversification of travel and tourism infrastructure, increased use by offenders of mobile technologies and the preponderance of domestic or intra-regional travelling offenders. However, each region faces its own particular challenges in relation to SECTT.

East Asia

Most tourists across East Asia are from within the region; domestic travelers far outnumber foreign tourists and SECTT appears to be dominated by Asian men. Business travel is increasingly accompanied by the rise of a corporate culture involving participation in after-hours "meetings" characterised

India Tops List of Traffickers of Women

India has been named the most dangerous country for women in terms of human trafficking according to a new Thomson Reuters Foundation survey of 550 experts on women's issues.

The survey asked respondents which 5 of the 193 United Nations member states they believed to be most dangerous for women and which country was the worst in terms of healthcare, economic resources, cultural or traditional practices, sexual violence and harassment, non-sexual violence, and human trafficking.

India was ranked the worst for human trafficking—encompassing domestic servitude, forced labor, bonded labor, forced marriage, and sexual slavery. India's Ministry of Women and Child Development declined to comment on rankings.

Thomson Reuters Foundation reports:

India, Libya and Myanmar were considered the world's most dangerous nations for women exploited by human traffickers in a global crime worth an estimated $150 billion a year.

"In many countries the simple fact of being female creates a heightened risk of becoming a victim of slavery," said Nick Grono,

by alcohol and sex. Inconsistent laws, definitions of children and interpretations of "consent" in different countries of the region undermine the coordination and collaboration necessary to find and convict offenders. Many responses focus on trafficking and countries have low rates of prosecution for the sexual abuse and exploitation of children.

Europe
Europe remains the number one tourist destination, welcoming more than half of the world's tourists in 2013, and there are suggestions that children's vulnerability to SECTT is on the rise. Western European countries have long been sources of travelling child sex offenders (TCSOs), but some are now destinations. Countries in Central and Eastern Europe are emerging as source

chief executive of the Freedom Fund, the first private donor fund dedicated to ending slavery.

The poll of 548 people was conducted online, by phone and in person between March 26 and May 4 with an even spread across Europe, Africa, the Americas, South East Asia, South Asia and the Pacific.

Respondents included aid professionals, academics, healthcare staff, non-government organisation workers, policy-makers, development specialists and social commentators.

Manjunath Gangadhara, an official at the Karnataka state government, lamented India's ranking, saying the country has shown utter disregard and disrespect for women.

"The (world's) fastest growing economy and leader in space and technology is shamed for violence committed against women."

Rounding out the top 10 worst countries for trafficking of women were Nigeria, Russia, the Philippines, Afghanistan, Thailand, Nepal, Pakistan, and Bangladesh.

Notably, the only Western nation ranked in the top 10 lists was the United States, which came in third on the list of worst countries for sexual violence against women.

"India Tops Rankings of Most Dangerous Countries for Trafficking of Women," Freedom United, June 26, 2018. Reprinted by permission.

and destination countries—often lacking the laws to protect children that exist elsewhere in the region. Regional institutions have adopted measures to enhance protection against child SECTT, which is sometimes addressed only within broader frameworks on violence or child protection.

Latin America

Tourist arrivals have quadrupled since 1980. While around three-quarters of all international visitors come from the USA and Canada, one study of four countries showed that the number of domestic travelers was double that of foreign tourists. Several countries and many households depend on revenue from tourism and travel, which increases the risk of SECTT for children and discourages reporting of the crime and the enforcement of relevant laws. Travel and tourism hotspots are often developed near poor and excluded communities, which can intensify disparities that expose children to SECTT: from income inequality to power imbalances.

Middle East and North Africa
The region faces specific challenges that heighten the risk of SECTT: conflict, wealth disparities that fuel migration, the low status of women and girls, harmful traditions such as child or "temporary" marriages and a lack of opportunities for youth. Some countries have been chastised by the Committee on the Rights of the Child for lacking information and awareness about SECTT and services to assist child victims. While countries have laws against child sexual exploitation, some still criminalise victims and the region lacks laws that are harmonised, allowing offenders to escape from one jurisdiction to another.

North America
Canada and the USA are source countries for offenders and, increasingly, destinations. Neither country maintains reliable data on SECTT, but there are signs that children are becoming involved at a younger age and that some engage in commercial sex for survival, with indigenous children at particular risk. A vast travel and tourism infrastructure is exploited by offenders, while traffickers supply child victims to meet the demand of business travelers attending conferences, and transient workers. The Internet and other technologies are widely used by victims.

The Pacific
The Pacific region, with its thousands of islands, has very limited data on SECTT. While Australia and New Zealand have well-established tourism and travel sectors and laws on child sexual exploitation, the Pacific Island Countries (PICs) are emerging destinations where awareness of the risks of SECTT and laws to address the crime are largely lacking. Children from indigenous communities seem particularly affected in Australia and New Zealand, while SECTT appears tied to specific activities in the

PICs: mining, logging and fishing. Social norms fuel the risks, including child marriage, tolerance of violence and commercial sex, children's low social status and taboos around sexual matters.

South Asia

South Asia is home to around half the world's poor, and tourism is a major source of income for some countries and communities. Domestic and regional travelers outnumber international visitors and social norms (such as gender discrimination) allow SECTT to flourish. Vulnerable boys tend to be involved in street-based sexual exploitation, while girls tend to be victimised in brothels and other sex venues. Booming access to mobile technology and the massive expansion of travel and tourism infrastructure, alongside a continuing lack of social safety nets, consistent definitions and effective legislation and enforcement, means that few offenders fear punishment and few victims receive the support they need.

Southeast Asia

In 2014, Southeast Asia had the fastest growth in tourism worldwide. SECTT by foreigners was first highlighted here, sparking global efforts to combat the crime. Traditional destinations such as Thailand and the Philippines still attract TCSOs, while Cambodia, Indonesia and Vietnam are becoming key destinations and Myanmar is at risk as it opens up to tourists. While the focus has long been on foreign tourists, male nationals account for the vast majority of offenders. Special Economic and Free Trade Zones in some countries have been identified as locations for SECTT and the region is seeing more webcam-based child sex tourism. No country has a specific plan or designated agency to tackle SECTT.

Sub-Saharan Africa

According to data from UNWTO, tourism in Africa has more than tripled in the last 20 years, and SECTT may be increasing, although empirical data are lacking. Increasingly diverse modes of travel and tourism attract visitors to once remote locations, and foreign direct investment is bringing in unaccompanied male workers. The region is seeing a surge in mobile data use, with mobile internet traffic expected to rise 20-fold by the end of the decade. Meanwhile, traditional norms continue to pose risks for children, particularly their low social status and child marriage conventions, but commitments have not translated into meaningful action for children and only a small percentage of child victims receive the help they need.

Key Global Findings

A number of global findings and conclusions emerge from the mass of evidence gathered for the Global Study.

The Spread of SECTT Reveals the Need for a Broader View

Twenty years ago, it might have been possible to sketch a rough global map showing where international travelling sex offenders were from, and where they were going. Today, the distinctions between countries of origin and countries of destination are blurring. Terms such as country of "origin," "destination" or "transit" are rapidly becoming outdated—countries can be any of these, or even all three, at different times. SECTT is now mainly a domestic and intra-regional crime, and can be found in both the world's most developed and least developed countries. What matters is where children are victimized and the Global Study finds that they are victimized everywhere.

Given that two decades of efforts have failed to put a dent in SECTT, that more children than ever before are being affected and that no country is immune, the Global Study highlights the need to re-frame this issue—looking beyond what was once referred to as "child sex tourism." This means broadening the scope of policies, programmes and research to include tourism and travel (whether international or domestic), and identifying and addressing what it is, exactly, about travel and tourism, that leaves children so vulnerable to exploitation.

Conclusion: The absence of a clear yet broad definition of SECTT has been an obstacle to effective responses. A proposed definition has emerged from the mass of research carried out for the Global Study over the past two years and should guide future efforts to combat SECTT:

> SECTT: Acts of sexual exploitation embedded in a context of travel, tourism, or both.

Tourism Is Soaring, While Child Protection Lags Behind

Tourism has seen extraordinary growth over the past 20 years, with the number of international tourist arrivals soaring from 527 million in 1995 to 1,135 million in 2014. While tourism development can bring enormous financial gains to countries, the private sector and local communities, evidence gathered for the Global Study suggests that the rush for tourist dollars poses a threat to children in the absence of measures to ensure their protection.

Conclusion: Tourism development plans must be informed by child-rights impact assessments and include measures to protect local children (based on consultations with local stakeholders, including children).

The Growth of Travel and Tourism Carries

The worldwide growth of travel and tourism has been accompanied by increasingly diverse *forms* of travel and tourism. New forms of travel have proliferated, such as tourism tied to volunteering (volun-tourism) and peer-to-peer arrangements for accommodation. These have multiplied the opportunities and venues available to offenders and thus the risk to children. Put simply: more people are on the move and more countries are competing for travel and tourism dollars, creating more opportunities for offenders to exploit children. At the same time, advances in Internet and mobile technology have contributed heavily to SECTT, allowing anonymity and hidden pathways for direct contact between offenders and victims. The private sector has a pivotal role to play in the solutions to SECTT—from prevention to awareness-raising, and from reporting to blocking the pathways exploited by offenders.

Conclusions: Efforts to involve the private sector in combatting SECTT need to be stepped up and should include not only multinational companies but small and medium-size businesses and individuals involved in tourism—such as guest houses, online marketplaces, zero-star hotels and taxi drivers. Collaboration is needed among information communication technology (ICT) companies and law enforcement agencies to block the use of new technologies for child sexual exploitation and disrupt financial gains for offenders, criminal networks and intermediaries, in collaboration with the financial industry.

There Is No Typical Victim

The research suggests that children from minority groups, boys and young children are far more vulnerable than previously understood, along with girls and children living in poverty. While stressing that child victims have no single story and come from a wide range of backgrounds and circumstances, the Global Study finds that they all have one thing in common: their vulnerability. Sadly, child victims cannot assume that society will offer them the support they need: services for their rescue, rehabilitation and recovery are inadequate the world over. These often hidden child victims need urgent help and real alternatives to build their future.

Conclusions: "One size fits all" approaches cannot hope to protect children against SECTT. Given that there is no "typical" victim, prevention and response measures must be tailored to the specific situation if they are to be effective. There must also be adequate resources to provide skilled care for child victims of SECTT.

There Is No Typical Offender

SECTT has become far more complex, involving not only tourists but business travelers, migrant/transient workers and "volun-tourists" intent on exploiting children, as well as large numbers of domestic travelers. The Global Study confirms that offenders can come from any background and that they do not all fit the stereotypical profile: a white, Western, wealthy middle-aged male paedophile. Some may be paedophiles, but most are not. Offenders may be foreign or domestic, young or old. Some are women, and a few may be other children. Research for the Global Study indicates that the majority are "situational" offenders—who may have never dreamed of sexually exploiting a child until given the opportunity to do so—rather than preferential offenders. The one thing both types of offenders have in common is ever-greater opportunities to exploit children, especially in environments where corruption is rife and impunity is the rule.

Conclusions: While not neglecting the need to pursue and prosecute the international preferential offenders who pose an ongoing threat to children, greater efforts are needed to tackle the situational, domestic and business travelers responsible for the vast majority of SECTT offences. The focus of SECTT research, policy, and action must, therefore, be expanded to include a much broader spectrum of travelers.

Power Imbalances Fuel SECTT

Offenders often use their comparative wealth and power to exploit children and evade justice. The Study finds that power imbalances between offenders and their victims play a critical role in SECTT; stereotyped attitudes toward children, gender and local cultures help to perpetuate the crime. At the same time, social tolerance of child sexual abuse and harmful cultural practices (such as child marriage and rigid definitions of masculinity) allow SECTT to thrive.

Conclusions: Reversing the power imbalances between offenders and their victims is beyond the scope of any single law, policy, institution or country, rooted as they are in hard-wired attitudes around wealth, gender, childhood and sexual dynamics. However, it is possible to tip the scales in favour of vulnerable children by, for example, raising community awareness about the dangers of SECTT, empowering children to enhance their resilience to sexual harm and ensuring that effective reporting mechanisms are in place and reports of SECTT are followed up. Strong stakeholder collaboration is needed as a matter of urgency for a global effort to inform the public about SECTT and turn tolerance into intolerance—a crucial step in ending this shameful crime.

Legislation Is Not Enough

Law enforcement efforts are undermined by weak laws to prohibit SECTT and lack of coordination among law enforcement agencies across the national jurisdictions. Most, if not all, countries have laws in place that should—at least in theory—protect children against sexual exploitation. Their enforcement, however, is hampered by the lack of a clear global definition of SECTT that is mirrored in national legislation, leaving police forces unsure about whether or how to prosecute. Enforcement is also hampered by chronic under-reporting, poor coordination across law enforcement agencies in different jurisdictions, and by a lack of understanding or urgency among some law enforcement agencies in different jurisdictions, and by a lack of understanding or urgency among some law enforcement officers.

Conclusions: Legal reforms that clearly define and prohibit SECTT are needed in all countries, along with increased resources for enforcement and greater (or improved) use of channels of information exchange, such as INTERPOL's Green Notices and national offender registries. Strenuous efforts are required to end impunity for offenders, build capacity in the justice sector and address corruption.

Data Gaps and Dilemmas Undermine the Response

The Global Study points to a number of serious data gaps and dilemmas, from the sheer difficulties of gathering data on the scale and scope to the absence of a clear definition of the crime and, therefore, a lack of clarity on what is to be measured. This lack of hard data matters immensely, as it makes it difficult to prioritise scarce resources or identify what works, and allows governments and societies to continue to ignore the problem. The absence of clear baselines and effective ways to monitor progress also undermines efforts to evaluate the impact of anti-SECTT programmes, posing a risk of donor disillusion and fatigue.

Conclusions: Data collection by national governments is essential to gauge the scale of SECTT and reveal the urgent need for domestic responses. The establishment of national systems capable of providing robust data and indicators on SECTT is the first step. Best practices should be identified and disseminated, alongside clear indicators and criteria to show what success looks like.

What Works: Effective Responses Need to Be Replicated and Scaled Up

The Study has demonstrated that efforts are underway to tackle SECTT and the approaches that are having some success. What seems to work is a comprehensive approach that mobilises a wide range of stakeholders—from government ministries to the general public—backed by good data. Countries that have addressed SECTT as part of a broader response to child sexual exploitation, focusing on prevention as well as response, seem to have had the greatest success. Efforts supported by bilateral and multilateral organisations and networks have been crucial, and international and regional cooperation has helped to overcome reluctance to acknowledge the problem. But it is impossible to overstate the importance of local prevention, local reporting and local responses.

Another important contribution of the Global Study is its increased focus on situational and domestic offenders, who account for most cases of SECTT, and on business travelers as well as tourists—a welcome shift from traditional approaches focusing solely on international preferential offenders.

Next Steps

The Global Study has revealed a set of specific tasks to be carried out by those with responsibility for the well-being of children, from international and regional organisations and national governments to the grass-roots groups working to protect children in local communities. There are also recommendations for the private sector, including not only companies directly involved in travel, tourism and transportation, but also those working in information communications technology and those whose staff members travel for business. Cross-sectoral recommendations point to the importance of coordinated approaches for effective SECTT prevention and intervention.

International and regional organisations, for example, are urged to place the commercial sexual exploitation of children higher on their political agendas, and meet their international commitments to protect children. National governments should, as a minimum, ratify and implement all international child rights instruments and, wherever necessary, revise their national laws and strengthen law enforcement and international cooperation to ensure that SECTT can be addressed.

Non-governmental organisations can monitor SECTT and bridge gaps left by national governments by, for example, monitoring and researching local SECTT, empowering citizens to play a role in prevention, identifying best practices, supporting the recovery and rehabilitation of SECTT victims and exposing those involved in this crime.

Private companies can be key players in the fight against SECTT through their active involvement in the protection of children's rights. Travel, tourism and transportation firms, for example, could sign up to child protection codes such as the Code of Conduct for the Protection of Children against Sexual Exploitation in Travel and Tourism or—at a minimum—adopt and enforce explicit corporate policies against SECTT. All companies in the travel, tourism and transportation sphere could also sign the UNWTO Code of Ethics. Larger companies can help to their knowledge and expertise. Measures are also needed to ensure that volun-tourism organisations have strong child protection systems and codes of conduct in place.

The wider ICT industry needs to adopt and enforce explicit corporate policies against SECTT and ensure compliance with *Human Rights and Business Principles and Children's Rights and Business Principles*. ICT companies can take a lead on the development of technology-based solutions to combat SECTT, such as blocking payment for SECTT-related offences and new techniques to "follow the money" and undermine the business model of SECTT offenders and their intermediaries.

Looking still wider, every company that sends its employees on business travel could arrange travel via child safe travel and tourism businesses and educate its employees on acceptable conduct and the need to protect children against SECTT. This could include the adoption and implementation of codes of conduct for travelling employees and background checks and police clearances for staff members who will have contact with children during their business trip.

One major finding of the Global Study is that ad-hoc and siloed approaches cannot hope to tackle a crime that is so complex—with no typical victims or perpetrators—that is found everywhere and that is so multi-faceted. Cross-sectoral partnerships and aligned approaches are essential to expand the impact of SECTT prevention and interventions, creating interventions that are coordinated and comprehensive rather than piecemeal. Partners across sectors should, as a first step, come together for a high-visibility global campaign to push for effective laws, strong enforcement, better protection of child victims and the end of impunity for offenders.

Finally, the Global Study has generated its own research agenda, which confirms that we need to know far more about every aspect of SECTT—its scale and scope (starting with baseline information), its victims, its perpetrators, its drivers and effective responses—if we are to stop it from spreading still further.

In Russia, Forms of Human Trafficking Such as Forced Labor and Sexual Exploitation Are Especially Virulent

The Minderoo Foundation

In the following excerpted viewpoint taken from The Global Slavery Index, a report produced by the Minderoo Foundation, Russia is highlighted as a country with a high prevalence of trafficking-related offenses, including forced labor, state-sanctioned forced labor, sexual trafficking, forced marriage, sexual exploitation of children and abuse of migrants and immigrants. Reasons and special conditions within the region such as governmental corruption and continuing war with neighboring countries, encouraging and creating conditions conducive to human trafficking, are explored. The Minderoo Foundation was founded in 2001 and has supported over 250 initiatives within Australia and internationally.

As you read, consider the following questions:

1. Why would a country such as Russia have such a high rate of human trafficking? What conditions contribute to this?
2. How does state imposed forced labor differ from officially illegal forced labor and what are additional problems in combating it?
3. What are some special challenges immigrants to Russia face regarding human trafficking exploitation?

"The Global Slavery Index 2018," The Minderoo Foundation. Reprinted by permission.

The Global Slavery Index estimates that 794,000 people lived in conditions of modern slavery in Russia on any given day in 2016, reflecting a prevalence rate of 5.5 victims for every thousand people.

The latest statistics provided by the United Nations Office on Drugs and Crime (UNODC), based on statistics collected by the Russian government, show that in 2015, there were 285 detected victims of trafficking under the different trafficking-related articles[1] of Russia's criminal code. Eighty-three of those were confirmed as victims of trafficking in persons and slave labour, and 202 were child victims of trafficking or other types of sexual exploitation.[2] The number of cases investigated for trafficking in persons and other related offences under those criminal code articles amounted to 2,717. Additionally, 1,473 individuals were prosecuted, and 1,196 individuals were convicted for trafficking or trafficking-related offences in 2015.[3]

Forced Labour

Forced labour in Russia predominantly occurs in informal and less regulated industries. Forms of labour exploitation can be found in a variety of sectors, such as agriculture, construction, domestic work, begging, trash collection, and illegal logging.[4] Forced labour involves migrant workers, who are either already in the country (including irregular migrants[5]), or foreign citizens who are brought to Russia for the purpose of exploitation.[6] Migrant workers who fall victim to exploitation primarily originate from Central Asian countries (such as Uzbekistan, Kazakhstan, and Tajikistan), Ukraine, Vietnam, China, and North Korea.[7]

There were documented cases of exploitation of construction workers working on stadium sites for the 2018 FIFA Soccer World Cup.[8] Research conducted by Human Rights Watch identified a range of abuses among these construction labourers, including non-payment and delayed payment of wages, as well as lack of employment contracts and other documentation required for legal employment.[9] Workers also reported having to work outside in extremely cold temperatures and facing retaliation or threats for raising concerns about their labour conditions. Seventeen workers have reportedly died on World Cup stadium sites in Russia.[10]

Internal migrants from Russia's poorer regions and migrants from the former Soviet satellite states are reportedly trafficked (sometimes involving drugging and kidnapping) and then forced to work against their will in brick factories and small farms in the North Caucasus republic of Dagestan.[11] This involves unscrupulous recruiters who target migrants at train stations in major Russian cities. These migrants come to Russia searching for work and are tricked into forced labour by recruiters offering fraudulent employment opportunities,[12] but then kidnapped or drugged and brought to far away Russian republics, such as Dagestan, where they are forced to work against their will.[13] There are also reports of workers from Ukraine[14] and Myanmar[15] who have experienced forced labour in Russia's fishing sector, involving recruitment agencies that deceived these workers about their working conditions.

Children exploited in forced begging is also increasingly an issue.[16] This type of forced labour mainly occurs in large cities. Victims are lured by promises of jobs, brought to the cities from other Russian provinces or foreign countries and then forced to beg in the streets. If they do not bring back a certain amount of money a day, they may be punished.[17]

State-Imposed Forced Labour

Compulsory prison labour was re-introduced as a criminal punishment from January 2017.[18] Under the current legislation, convicted prisoners may be forced to perform labour at state prisons or private companies. Although prisoners' working conditions are technically covered by general labour laws, the voluntary consent of the prisoner to perform such work is not required. Therefore, there are concerns that prisoners are forced to work for private companies against their will.[19] In addition, Russian law allows for compulsory labour to be imposed as a punishment for various activities, including the expression of political or ideological views which are deemed to be "extremist." The definition of "extremist activities" is vague, which could therefore result in arbitrary imprisonment involving compulsory labour.[20] Recent amendments to the law also allow changing the punishment from compulsory labour to a prison sentence if the convict evades the conviction or violates the regime of compulsory works.[21]

In early 2018, following the adoption of UN Security Council (UNSC) Resolution 2375 on 11 September, asking that all UN member states ban North Korean migrant labour,[22] and adoption of UNSC Resolution 2397 on 22 December 2017, demanding the repatriation of all North Korean migrant workers working overseas,[23] the Russian government reportedly began repatriating North Koreans who had previously entered Russia under a labour agreement between the two countries.[24] North Koreans who were previously sent to Russia under this agreement were reportedly subject to forced labour, including seized wages to cover living expenses and other "mandatory contributions," which are an ongoing source of income for the regime in Pyongyang.[25] It is estimated that more than 50,000 North Korean migrant workers have been sent abroad through the North Korean state-sponsored system, most of whom were sent to Russia and China. Once overseas, North Korean migrant workers are primarily employed in the mining, logging, textile, and construction industries.[26] Workers often do not know the details of their employment contract, parts of their salaries are withheld, and they are forced to work up to 20 hours per day.[27] In 2017, allegations of North Korean migrant workers being exploited in the construction of the St. Petersburg World Cup stadium emerged,[28] which FIFA later confirmed.[29]

Forced Sexual Exploitation of Adults and Children

Russian women and children are victims of forced sexual exploitation, both within Russia and overseas. Additionally, foreign women from Europe (mainly Ukraine and Moldova), Southeast Asia (primarily Vietnam), Africa (mainly Nigeria), and Central Asia fall victim to sex trafficking within Russia.[30] There are reports of Nigerian women and girls being trafficked to Russia on student visas and subsequently forced into sex work to repay their alleged "debts" for visa and travel costs. The victims are allegedly officially accepted into universities in Russia so that they may obtain their visa document, but rarely make contact with the universities once they had arrived in Russia.[31]

Child commercial sexual exploitation is prevalent throughout Russia, although the visibility of the crime has decreased due to an upsurge in internet usage, which has created new pathways to approach and exploit victims. It is reported that teenage girls are primarily sexually exploited in brothels, hostels, saunas, and increasingly in private apartments.[32]

Forced Marriage

There are reports of Russian women and girls being abducted for forced marriage in the northern Caucasus region.[33] In 2015, the case of a 17-year-old girl who was reportedly forced into marrying a 46-year-old police commander in Chechnya in the northern Caucasus received international media attention.[34] The police chief took the girl as his second wife although polygamy is prohibited in Russia, but apparently common in Chechnya.[35]

Imported Products at Risk of Modern Slavery

While Russia is affected by modern slavery within its own borders, the realities of global trade and business make it inevitable that Russia, like many other countries globally, will be exposed to the risk of modern slavery through the products it imports. Policymakers, businesses, and consumers must become aware of this risk and take responsibility for it. Table 1 below highlights the top five products (according to US$ value, per annum) imported by Russia that are at risk of being produced under conditions of modern slavery.[36]

Table 1. Imports of Products at Risk of Modern Slavery to Russia

Product at risk of modern slavery	Import value (in thousands of US$)	Source countries
Laptops, computers and mobile phones	3,884,695	China, Malaysia
Apparel and clothing accessories	3,025,133	Argentina, Brazil, China, India, Malaysia, Thailand, Vietnam
Cattle	917,523	Brazil, Paraguay
Sugarcane	321,834	Brazil
Fish	249,360	China, Indonesia, Japan, South Korea, Taiwan, Thailand

The highest value at-risk products that may be produced using modern slavery and imported by Russia are laptops, computers, and mobile phones, and apparel. In fact, over 60 percent (corresponding to a value of US$ 3.8 billion) of all laptops, computers and mobile phones imported by Russia are from China, which is considered at risk of using modern slavery in the production of these goods. Similarly, of the more than US$ 3 billion worth of clothing from various at-risk countries, nearly US$ 2.7 billion come from China. Cattle from Brazil and Paraguay are the third largest import to Russia that may be produced using modern slavery (US$ 917.5 million). Russia imports 85 percent of its sugarcane from Brazil, totaling US\$ 321.8 million in value. Fish from various at-risk countries are imported into Russia up to an annual value of US\$ 249.4 million. Fish imports from China make up by far the largest share of these fish imports (nearly US\$ 178 million).

Vulnerability

Xenophobia, intolerance, and negative attitudes toward migrant workers,[37] asylum seekers[38] and marginalised groups, such as the LGBTQI community,[39] exposes these populations to increased risk of exploitation and abuse in Russia. For example, in 2017, brutal campaigns against gay men in Chechnya reportedly led to abduction, forced disappearances, torture, and deaths by authorities.[40]

The large majority of Russia's migrant workers are irregular migrants[41]—a status that can make them particularly vulnerable to modern slavery. An estimated 10 to 12 million workers enter Russia annually.[42] After the collapse of the Soviet Union, civil war and increasingly repressive regimes caused many individuals from the Central Asian republics to move to Russia in search of employment, taking advantage of visa-free travel arrangements. Once in Russia these individuals faced physical abuse, withholding of documents, and unsafe working conditions.[43] In recent years, the trouble has been devalued amid the contraction of the Russian economy due to low crude oil prices and western sanctions in response to Russia's annexation of Crimea and involvement in Eastern Ukraine.[44] In light of this and increasingly negative public and government attitudes towards migrants from Central Asia[45]—combined with more restrictive migration policies aimed at Tajik, Belarusian, Kazak, and Armenian citizens[46]—more migrants from Central Asia are entering Russia irregularly and thereby are more vulnerable to exploitation.[47] Patterns exist where irregular migrants, due to their undocumented status, are willing to accept jobs without knowing exactly the nature and conditions of the work they are committing to.

The conflict in the eastern part of the neighbouring Ukraine has increased the risk of cross-border trafficking and forced labour due to war, displacement, and economic crisis.[48] Ukraine has one of the largest diasporas in the world, with the major share residing in Russia.[49] Russia was one of the most popular destination countries for Ukrainian migrants seeking work abroad in 2014-15 despite the conflict, with 2.5 million Ukrainian citizens registered in Russia.[50] The main destination country of all Ukrainian victims of human trafficking who were provided with IOM assistance between 2010 and 2015 was Russia.[51] A survey commissioned by the IOM also found that the percentage of Ukrainians who would agree to precarious offers regarding working abroad increased from 14 percent in 2011 to 21 percent in 2015.[52] This may reflect a worsening economic situation and increasing conflict in the Ukraine.

Government corruption and complicity heightens vulnerability of Russian citizens and migrants to modern slavery. There have been reports of Russian government officials facilitating trafficking and entry of trafficking victims into Russia.[53] Some employers reportedly bribe Russian officials to avoid penalties imposed on them for employing irregular migrants.[54] There are also suspicions that officials charge migrant workers who enter the country excessive fees for work permits.[55]

There are strongly patriarchal views of marriage in some of Russia's republics in the North Caucasus, such as Dagestan and Chechnya.[56] These views are reinforced by cultural traditions and religious views that do not respect women's rights. Rules practiced in these regions contradict rights set out in the Russian Constitution and may contribute to women's vulnerability to forced marriage in these areas.[57]

Response to Modern Slavery

Russia has criminalised human trafficking in article 127.1 of the criminal code. While the use of slave labour is criminalised under article 127.2 and article 127.1 mentions slave labour as a type of exploitation as part of the crime of human trafficking, the act of slavery itself is not distinctly criminalised.[58] Articles 240 and 241 address recruitment into sex work and pimping.[59]

In relation to the alleged exploitation of migrant workers from North Korea on the construction site for the St Petersburg stadium for the 2018 Soccer World Cup, the St Petersburg construction committee reported that authorities had regularly conducted inspections to ensure Russian labour laws are respected.[60] Although Russia has a labour code and inspections are carried out under this basis, labour inspectors do not specifically target forced labour or rigorously investigate workers' complaints during their inspections. At the time of writing there had not been any criminal investigations as a result of labour inspections carried out on construction sites for the World Cup.[61]

New legislation that limits temporary agency work (known as "outstaffing" in Russia) came into effect in January 2016. The new law amends the labour code, tax code, and existing employment law.[62] It limits the amount of time an employer can send employees to work for other firms and requires these outsourced employees to earn the same amount as permanent employees.[63] Previously, companies were able to use temporary employers to carry out harmful or hazardous work without paying additional benefits, so this legislation may help reduce the vulnerability of these temporary workers.[64]

The Russian government has put tougher restrictions on migrant workers in an attempt to cut the number of irregular migrant workers in the country. At the beginning of 2015, a new law came into effect that requires foreign workers from countries that do not have a visa policy with Russia to obtain a license to be able to work legally, to pass Russian language and history tests, and pay extensive medical insurance and examination fees.[65] The new law has particularly affected migrant workers from CIS (Commonwealth of Independent States) countries, such as Tajikistan, who were previously able to use their national identity cards to enter and remain in Russia, but now need to produce an international passport instead.[66] This law has resulted in a slight decline in influxes of migrant labour in 2016-2017, but—despite concerns[67]—it is unclear if it drove considerable amounts of workers underground or prevented them from coming to Russia altogether.

A new extradition agreement between Russia and North Korea, signed in February 2016, introduced measures to allow mutual deportation of illegal immigrants.[68] The Main Directorate for Migration Affairs (until April 2016, previously called the Federal Migration Service) is now allowed to repatriate North Koreans who are "illegally" residing in Russia, even though they may face serious risk of abuse and exploitation in labour camps, or even the death penalty, upon their return to North Korea. There are concerns that this may also affect those North Koreans with refugee or asylum seeker status in Russia.[69] In addition, the repatriation of North Korean migrant workers as a result of the sanctions under UN Security Council Resolution 2397[70] could expose those repatriated workers to exploitation in their home country.

A 2012 law, which demanded that foreign-financed NGOs and other international organisations that engaged in political activities register as "foreign agents" was further amended in 2014 to authorise the Justice Ministry to register "undesirable groups" as "foreign agents," even without their consent.[71] This law effectively cracks down on civil society, including groups combatting modern slavery and providing support services for victims. Human Rights Watch reports that as of July 2017, the list of active "foreign agents" consisted of 88 groups.[72] At least one NGO that performs counselling for victims of trafficking and one NGO that assists migrants were added to this list.[73]

The Russian government provides no funding for dedicated shelters for modern slavery victims.[74] Limited shelter services are exclusively provided by a limited number of NGOs.[75] In major cities such as St Petersburg or Moscow, shelters for homeless people may take in trafficking victims on a case-by-case basis. There are shelters for women and children in distress in major cities, which are usually funded by municipalities, that can deal with modern slavery victims, although they are not specifically trained to care for these types of victims. Adolescent victims of trafficking are placed in shelters for children in distress.[76]

Generally, victims are identified and referred by either NGOs or law enforcement on an ad hoc basis. The Russian government has not yet introduced a comprehensive National Referral Mechanism (NRM), which would provide a framework for cooperation among the different actors involved in identifying and protecting victims.[77]

The Russian government re-introduced compulsory labour in its prison system, beginning 1 January 2017. Compulsory labour was originally included as a provision in the Russian Criminal Code in 2011 to offer an alternative punishment to prison, but its implementation had been postponed due to a lack of facilities.[78] Four new correctional facilities have recently opened, that will house criminals sentenced to compulsory labour. These facilities have lower security than prisons and allow convicted criminals to leave with permission from authorities. However, individuals will not be allowed to refuse or switch jobs once they are assigned to a role. It is reported that individuals subject to compulsory labour will receive a salary.[79] Starting in 2018, individuals who violate the regime of compulsory labour or try to evade it may also receive a higher penalty, such as a prison sentence.[80]

The Russian government did not draft a national action plan and failed to establish a body or similar measures to effectively coordinate the government's response to modern slavery.[81]

[…]

Notes

1. This refers to offences recorded under articles 120 (forced organ removal), 127.1 (trafficking in persons), 127.2 (slave labour), 240 and 241 (enticement into prostitution and pimping), 242.1 (production and circulation of material or objects with pornographic depiction of minors), and 242.2 (use of minors for the production of pornographic materials).
2. United Nations Office on Drugs and Crime 2016, "Global Report on Trafficking in Persons: Eastern Europe and Central Asia Country Profile," pp. 22-23. Available from: http://www.unodc.org/documents/data-and-analysis/glotip/Glotip16_Country_profile_E_EuropeCentral_Asia.pdf. [29 November 2017].
3. As above.

4. Maltseva, E., McCarthy, L., Mokhova, M., Poletaev, D., & Schenk, C. 2014, "Country Strategy Report: Modern Slavery Landscape in Russia" (draft), Walk Free Foundation, pp. 16-18.

5. Obrazkova, M. 2013, "Moscow Illegal Immigrants Also Victims of Exploitation." Russia Beyond, 16 August. Available from: https://www.rbth.com/politics/2013/08/16/is_moscow_facing_a_slavery_emergency_28965.html. [26 April 2018].

6. Maltseva, E., McCarthy, L., Mokhova, M., Poletaev, D., & Schenk, C. 2014, "Country Strategy Report: Modern Slavery Landscape in Russia" (draft), Walk Free Foundation.

7. As above.

8. Higgins, A. 2017, "North Korean's in Russia Work 'Basically in the Situation of Slaves.'" *New York Times*, 11 July. Available from: https://www.nytimes.com/2017/07/11/world/europe/north-korea-russia-migrants.html. [9 April 2018. Human Rights Watch 2017, "Red Card: Exploitation of Construction Workers on World Cup Sites in Russia." Available from: https://www.hrw.org/sites/default/files/report_pdf/russiafifa0617_web_0.pdf. [30 November 2017]. Levi Bridges 2017, "Many Migrant Workers Building Russia's World Cup Sites Are Getting Stiffed," Public Radio International, 3 July. Available from: https://www.pri.org/stories/2017-07-03/many-migrant-workers-building-russias-world-cup-sites-are-getting-stiffed. [26 April 2018].

9. Human Rights Watch 2017, "Red Card: Exploitation of Construction Workers on World Cup Sites in Russia." Available from: https://www.hrw.org/sites/default/files/report_pdf/russiafifa0617_web_0.pdf. [30 November 2017].

10. As above.

11. Hodal, K. 2017, "Slave Saviours: The Men Risking Their Lives to Free Brick Workers in Dagestan," *Guardian,* 1 April. Available from: https://www.theguardian.com/global-development/2017/apr/01/slave-saviours-men-risking-their-lives-to-free-brick-workers-in-dagestan. [9 April 2018].

12. Fomin, S. 2015, "Slavery in Modern Russia," Open Democracy, 1 June. Available from: https://www.opendemocracy.net/od-russia/stepan-fomin/slavery-in-modern-russia. [9 April 2018].

13. Hodal, K. 2017, "Slave Saviours: The Men Risking Their Lives to Free Brick Workers in Dagestan," *Guardian,* 1 April. Available from: https://www.theguardian.com/global-development/2017/apr/01/slave-saviours-men-risking-their-lives-to-free-brick-workers-in-dagestan. [9 April 2018].

14. Surtees, R. 2012, "Trafficked at Sea: The Exploitation of Ukrainian Seafarers and Fishers," International Organization for Migration & Nexus Institute. Available from: http://publications.iom.int/system/files/pdf/trafficked_at_sea_web.pdf. [28 March 2018].

15. Lone, W. and Barron, L. 2015, "Trawler Tragedy Lifts Veil on Illegal Recruitment," *Myanmar Times,* 7 April. Available from: https://www.mmtimes.com/national-news/13967-trawler-tragedy-lifts-veil-on-illegal-recruitment.html. [14 March 2018].

16. OSCE Special Representative and Co-ordinator for Combating Trafficking in Human Beings, Madina Jarbussynova, 2017. "Report by OSCE Special Representative and Co-ordinator for Combating Trafficking in Human Beings, Madina Jarbussynova," following her official visit to the Russian Federation, 6-11 February 2017. Organization for Security and Co-operation in Europe. Available from: https://www.osce.org/cthb/107636. [9 April 2018].

17. Maltseva, E., McCarthy, L., Mokhova, M., Poletaev, D., & Schenk, C. 2014, "Country Strategy Report: Modern Slavery Landscape in Russia" (draft), Walk Free Foundation.

18. Kovpak, J. 2016, "Russia to Reintroduce Forced Labor as Criminal Punishment," Voice of America, 13 October. Available from: https://www.voanews.com/a/russia-forced-labor/3549099.html. [28 March 2018].

19. International Labour Organization Committee of Experts 2017, direct request (CEACR)—Adopted 2016, published 106th ILC session (2017), Forced Labour Convention, 1930 (No. 29)—Russian Federation (Ratification: 1956), International Labour Organization. Available from: http://www.ilo.org/dyn/normlex/en/f?p=NOR MLEXPUB:13100:0::NO::P13100_COMMENT_ID:3299906, [26 April 2018].

20. International Labour Organization Committee of Experts 2017, Observation (CEACR)—adopted 2016, published 106th ILC session (2017), Abolition of Forced Labour Convention, 1957 (No. 105)—Russian Federation (Ratification: 1998), International Labour Organization. Available from: http://www.ilo.org/dyn/normlex/en/f?p=1000:13100:0::NO:13100:P13100_COMMENT_ID,P11110_COUNTRY_ID,P11110_COUNTRY_NAME,P11110_COMMENT_YEAR:3298628,102884,Russian%20Federation,2016. [26 April 2018].

21. Президент России 2018, Федеральный закон от 23.04.2018 № 96-ФЗ: О внесении изменений в статью 53–1 Уголовного кодекса Российской Федерации и Уголовно-процессуальный кодекс Российской Федерации [President of Russia 2018, Federal Law No. 96-FZ of April 23, 2018 On Amending Article 53-1 of the Criminal Code of the Russian Federation and the Code of Criminal Procedure of the Russian Federation].Available from: http://kremlin.ru/acts/bank/42974. [2 May 2018].

22. United Nations Security Council 2017, Resolution 2375 (2017), United Nations, 11 September. Available from: https://www.un.org/ga/search/view_doc.asp?symbol=S/RES/2375%282017%29. [17 May 2018].

23. United Nations Security Council 2017, Security Council Tightens Sanctions on Democratic People's Republic of Korea, Unanimously Adopting Resolution 2397 (2017), United Nations, 22 December. Available from: https://www.un.org/press/en/2017/sc13141.doc.htm. [6 February 2017].

24. "Russia Begins Deportation of North Korean Workers—Ambassador" 2018, TASS Russian News Agency, 7 February. Available from: http://tass.com/politics/988788. [2 May 2018], "Russia to Send Home All North Korean Migrant Workers by 2019: Ifax" 2018, Thomson Reuters, 31 January. Available from: https://www.reuters.com/article/us-northkorea-missiles-russia-sanctions/russia-to-send-home-all-north-korean-migrant-workers-by-2019-ifax-idUSKBN1FJ2RZ. [2 May 2018].

25. Higgins, A. 2017, "North Koreans in Russia Work 'Basically in the Situation of Slaves,'" *New York Times*, 11 July. Available from: https://www.nytimes.com/2017/07/11/world/europe/north-korea-russia-migrants.html. [9 April 2018].

26. United Nations Secretary-General 2015, "Situation of Human Rights in the Democratic People's Republic of Korea." United Nations General Assembly, Seventieth session, p. 6. Available from: https://reliefweb.int/sites/reliefweb.int/files/resources/N1527317.pdf. [29 March 2018].

27. As above, pp. 6-7.

28. Luhn, A. 2017, "'Like Prisoners of War': North Korean Labour Behind Russia 2018 World Cup," *The Guardian*, 4 June. Available from: https://www.theguardian.com/football/2017/jun/04/like-prisoners-of-war-north-korean-labour-russia-world-cup-st-petersburg-stadium-zenit-arena. [29 November 2017].

29. Conn, D. 2017, "World Cup 2018: FIFA Admits Workers Have Suffered Human Rights Abuses," *The Guardian*, 25 May. Available from: https://www.theguardian.com/football/2017/may/25/fifa-world-cup-2018-workers-human-rights-abuses. [26 April 2018].

30. Office to Monitor and Combat Trafficking in Persons 2017, "Trafficking in Persons Report: Russia Country Narrative," United States Department of State. Available from: https://www.state.gov/documents/organization/271344.pdf. [30 November 2017].

31. Burrows, E. 2016, "How Nigerian Girls Are Forced into Prostitution in Russia," Deutsche Welle, 21 April. Available from: http://www.dw.com/en/how-nigerian-girls-are-forced-into-prostitution-in-russia/a-19201378. [9 April 2018].

32. Russian Alliance against CSEC & ECPAT International 2017, "Submission on Sexual Exploitation of Children in the Russian Federation for the Universal Periodic Review of the Human Rights Situation in the Russian Federation" (UPR third cycle 2017 – 2021), 2 October. Available from: http://www.ecpat.org/wp-content/uploads/2017/09/Russia-UPR-Report-2017.docx. [9 April 2018].

33. Committee on the Elimination of Discrimination against Women 2015, "Concluding Observations on the Eighth Periodic Report of the Russian Federation," United Nations Office of the High Commissioner. Available from: http://www.ohchr.org/EN/Issues/Slavery/SRSlavery/Pages/CountryVisits.aspx. [30 November 2017].

34. "Russia 'Forced Marriage' Reporter Milashina Flees Chechnya," 2015, BBC News, 14 May. Available from: http://www.bbc.com/news/world-europe-32745569. [9 April 2018]., Lokshina, T. 2015, "Dispatches: Will Russia Protect a Child Bride?," Human Rights Watch, 13 May. Available from: https://www.hrw.org/news/2015/05/13/dispatches-will-russia-protect-child-bride. [9 April 2018].

35. Greenslade, R. 2015, "Russia's Independent Newspaper Reveals Forced Marriage in Chechnya," *The Guardian*, 18 May. Available from: https://www.theguardian.com/media/greenslade/2015/may/18/russias-independent-newspaper-reveals-forced-marriage-in-chechnya. [9 April 2018].

36. "The Top Five Imported Products at Risk of Modern Slavery Were Identified from an Original List of 15 Products Considered at Risk of Modern Slavery." For a detailed methodology of how these products were identified, please refer to Appendix 3 in the 2018 GSI report. The data is taken from the BACI 2015 dataset (available from: http://www.cepii.fr/cepii/en/bdd_modele/presentation.asp?id=1).

37. Sinelschikova, Y. 2017, "Distinguishing Faces: What Do Russians Think about Migrants?," Russia Beyond, 18 May. Available from: https://www.rbth.com/politics_and_society/2017/05/18/distinguishing-faces-what-do-russians-think-about-migrants_765076. [10 April 2018].

38. Kislov, D., and Zhanaev, E. 2017, "Russia: Xenophobia and Vulnerability of Migrants from Central Asia," The Foreign Policy Centre, 4 December. Available from: https://fpc.org.uk/russia-xenophobia-vulnerability-migrants-central-asia/. [10 April 2018].

39. Kondakov, A. 2017, "Putting Russia's Homophobia Violence on the Map," Open Democracy, 17 May. Available from: https://www.opendemocracy.net/od-russia/alexander-kondakov/putting-russia-s-homophobic-violence-on-map. [25 June 2018].

40. Knight, K. 2017, "Gay Men in Chechnya Are Being Tortured and Killed. More Will Suffer If We Don't Act," *The Guardian*, 13 April. Available from: https://www.theguardian.com/commentisfree/2017/apr/13/gay-men-targeted-chechnya-russia. [10 April 2018], Amnesty International n.d., "Chechnya: Stop Abducting and Killing Gay Men." Available from: https://www.amnesty.org/en/get-involved/take-action/chechnya-stop-abducting-and-killing-gay-men/. [2 May 2018].

41. Balforth, T. 2013, "Russia's Migrant-Worker Underclass," *The Atlantic*. Available from: https://www.theatlantic.com/international/archive/2013/01/russias-migrant-worker-underclass/267144/. [26 April 2018].

42. Eke, S. n.d., "Russia: New Rules Hit Foreign Workers," BBC World Service, World Agenda. Available from: http://www.bbc.co.uk/worldservice/specials/119_wag_climate/page9.shtml. [01 May 2018]. See also: Najibullah, F 2014, 'Russia to test migrant workers on country's history,' Radio Free Europe, 13 June. Available from: https://www.rferl.org/a/russia-migrants-history-tests-25420832.html. [1 May 2018].

43. Kislov, D., & Zhanaev, E. 2017, "Russia: Xenophobia and Vulnerability of Migrants from Central Asia," The Foreign Policy Centre, 4 December. Available from: https://fpc.org.uk/russia-xenophobia-vulnerability-migrants-central-asia/. [27 April 2018]. See also: Matusevich, Y. 2017, "Russia, Xenophobia and Profiting from Migration Controls," News Deeply, 3 August. Available from: https://www.newsdeeply.com/refugees/community/2017/08/03/russia-xenophobia-and-profiting-from-migration-controls. [27 April 2018].

44. Hille, K. 2018, "Russia's Economy: Challenges Facing Vladimir Putin," *The Financial Times,* 28 February. Available from: https://www.ft.com/content/3aac3faa-1bb6-11e8-aaca-4574d7dabfb6. [27 April 2018].

45. Kislov, D., & Zhanaev, E. 2017, 'Russia: Xenophobia and Vulnerability of Migrants from Central Asia," The Foreign Policy Centre, 4 December. Available from: https://fpc.org.uk/russia-xenophobia-vulnerability-migrants-central-asia/. [27 April 2018].

46. Umarova, I., & Sujud, J 2015, "Tajiks Face New Obstacles to Work in Russia," Institute for War and Peace Reporting (IWPR). Available from: https://iwpr.net/global-voices/tajiks-face-new-obstacles-work-russia. [27 April 2018].

47. Schottenfeld, J. 2017, "The Midnight Train to Moscow," Foreign Policy, 10 August. Available from: http://foreignpolicy.com/2017/08/10/the-midnight-train-to-moscow-tajikistan-migration/. [27 April 2018].

48. Dean, L. A. 2016, "The Other Victims of the War in Ukraine," Atlantic Council, 11 October. Available from: http://www.atlanticcouncil.org/blogs/ukrainealert/human-trafficking-consequences-of-the-war-in-ukraine. [10 April 2018].

49. International Organization for Migration, "Mission in Ukraine, 2016, Migration in Ukraine: Facts and Figures," p. 17. Available from: http://www.iom.org.ua/sites/default/files/ff_eng_10_10_press.pdf. [10 April 2018].

50. As above, p. 13.

51. As above, p. 30.

52. GfK Ukraine 2015, "Human Trafficking Survey: Ukraine," International Organization for Migration. Available from: http://www.iom.org.ua/sites/default/files/pres_gfk_iom2015_ukraine_eng_fin_3_2.pdf. [10 April 2018].

53. Office to Monitor and Combat Trafficking in Persons 2017, "Trafficking in Persons Report: Russia Country Narrative." United States Department of State. Available from: https://www.state.gov/documents/organization/271344.pdf. [30 November 2017]., Burrows, E. 2016, "How Nigerian Girls Are Forced into Prostitution in Russia," Deutsche Welle, 21 April. Available from: http://www.dw.com/en/how-nigerian-girls-are-forced-into-prostitution-in-russia/a-19201378. [9 April 2018].

54. Office to Monitor and Combat Trafficking in Persons 2017, "Trafficking in Persons Report: Russia Country Narrative." United States Department of State. Available from: https://www.state.gov/documents/organization/271344.pdf. [30 November 2017].

55. Chizhova, L., & Kurachyova, O. 2013, "Behind Russia's Migrant Raids, a Vast Network of Bribes and Opportunism," *The Atlantic*, 8 August. Available from: https://www.theatlantic.com/international/archive/2013/08/behind-russias-migrant-raids-a-vast-network-of-bribes-and-opportunism/278481/. [10 April 2018].

56. Maltseva, E, McCarthy, L, Mokhova, M, Poletaev, D & Schenk, C 2014, Country Strategy Report: Modern Slavery Landscape in Russia (draft), Walk Free Foundation.

57. Vityazeva, A. 2015, "Women's Rights Squeezed in North Caucasus Amid Revival of Muslim Traditions," Russia Beyond, 16 June. Available from: https://www.rbth.com/society/2015/06/16/womens_rights_squeezed_in_north_caucasus_amid_revival_of_muslim_tradi_46939.html. [9 April 2018].

58. OSCE Office for Democratic Institutions and Human Rights, n.d., "Criminal Code of the Russian Federation" (1996, amended 2012) (English version), Legislation Online. Available from: http://legislationline.org/documents/section/criminal-codes/country/7. [2 May 2018].

59. United Nations Office on Drugs and Crime 2016, "Global Report on Trafficking in Persons: Eastern Europe and Central Asia Country Profile," p.22. Available from: http://www.unodc.org/documents/data-and-analysis/glotip/Glotip16_Country_profile_E_EuropeCentral_Asia.pdf. [29 November 2017]. An English translation of the Russian Criminal Code is also available from: http://legislationline.org/documents/section/criminal-codes/country/7. [29 November 2017].

60. Luhn, A. 2017, "'Like Prisoners of War': North Korean Labour Behind Russia 2018 World Cup," *The Guardian,* 4 June. Available from: https://www.theguardian.com/football/2017/jun/04/like-prisoners-of-war-north-korean-labour-russia-world-cup-st-petersburg-stadium-zenit-arena. [29 November 2017].

61. Personal communication.

62. "Russia: Significant Labor Law Changes for 2016 Will Alter Temporary Employee Market" 2014, Willis Towers Watson. Available from: https://www.towerswatson.com/en/Insights/Newsletters/Global/global-news-briefs/2014/06/russia-2016-labor-law-changes-will-affect-temporary-workers. [30 November 2017].

63. Office to Monitor and Combat Trafficking in Persons 2017, "Trafficking in Persons Report: Russia Country Narrative." United States Department of State. Available from: https://www.state.gov/documents/organization/271344.pdf. [30 November 2017].

64. Antipkina, O. 2017, "Regulation of Secondment (Outstaffing) in Russia," Lexology. Available from: https://www.lexology.com/library/detail.aspx?g=f9afced8-f038-4c21-ab80-5a5052d08da0. [30 November 2017].

65. Sinelschikova, Y. 2014, "Changes to Migration Regulations Aim to Legalize Shadow Workers," Russia Beyond, 5 December. Available from: https://www.rbth.com/arts/2014/12/05/changes_to_migration_regulations_aim_to_legalize_shadow_workers_42011.html. [11 December 2017].

66. Russia Beyond 2014, "Russia Toughens Migration Policy for CIS Citizens." 24 June. Available from: https://www.rbth.com/news/2014/06/24/russia_toughens_migration_policy_for_cis_citizens_37673.html. [11 December 2017].

67. Sinelschikova, Y. 2014, "Changes to Migration Regulations Aim to Legalize Shadow Workers," Russia Beyond, 5 December. Available from: https://www.rbth.com/arts/2014/12/05/changes_to_migration_regulations_aim_to_legalize_shadow_workers_42011.html. [11 December 2017].

68. Tumanov, G. 2016, "Moscow Agrees to Repatriate Illegal North Korean Immigrants," Russia Beyond, 11 February. Available from: https://www.rbth.com/international/2016/02/11/bleak-future-awaits-north-korean-deportees-from-russia_566735. [30 November 2017].

69. Kim, J., & Macfie, N. 2015, "U.N. Envoy Says Russia-North Korea Deportation Pact Puts Refugees at Risk," Thomson Reuters, 26 November. Available from: https://www.reuters.com/article/us-northkorea-russia-un/u-n-envoy-says-russia-north-korea-deportation-pact-puts-refugees-at-risk-idUSKBN0TF10120151126. [30 November 2017].

70. "Russia Begins Deportation of North Korean Workers—Ambassador" 2018, TASS Russian News Agency, 7 February. Available from: http://tass.com/politics/988788. [2 May 2018], "Russia to Send Home All North Korean Migrant Workers by 2019: Ifax" 2018, Thomson Reuters, 31 January. Available from: https://www.reuters.com/article/us-northkorea-missiles-russia-sanctions/russia-to-send-home-all-north-korean-migrant-workers-by-2019-ifax-idUSKBN1FJ2RZ. [2 May 2018].

71. Human Rights Watch 2017, "Russia: Government vs. Rights Groups," 8 September. Available from: https://www.hrw.org/russia-government-against-rights-groups-battle-chronicle. [8 December 2017], Luhn, A. 2015, "Russia Bans 'Undesirable' International Organisations Ahead of 2016 Elections," *The Guardian*, 19 May. Available from: https://www.theguardian.com/world/2015/may/19/russia-bans-undesirable-international-organisations-2016-elections. [8 December 2017].

72. Human Rights Watch 2017, "Russia: Government vs. Rights Groups," 8 September. Available from: https://www.hrw.org/russia-government-against-rights-groups-battle-chronicle. [8 December 2017].

73. Personal communication.

74. Office to Monitor and Combat Trafficking in Persons 2017, "Trafficking in Persons Report: Russia Country Narrative." United States Department of State. Available from: https://www.state.gov/documents/organization/271344.pdf. [30 November 2017].

75. OSCE Special Representative and Co-ordinator for Combating Trafficking in Human Beings, Madina Jarbussynova, 2017, Report by OSCE Special Representative and Co-ordinator for Combating Trafficking in Human Beings, Madina Jarbussynova, following her official visit to the Russian Federation, 6-11 February 2017. Organization for Security and Co-operation in Europe. Available from: https://www.osce.org/cthb/107636. [9 April 2018]., p. 9.

76. Field source.

77. OSCE Special Representative and Co-ordinator for Combating Trafficking in Human Beings, Madina Jarbussynova, 2017, Report by OSCE Special Representative and Co-ordinator for Combating Trafficking in Human Beings, Madina Jarbussynova, following her official visit to the Russian Federation, 6-11 February 2017. Organization for Security and Co-operation in Europe, p. 8. Available from: https://www.osce.org/cthb/107636. [9 April 2018].

78. Kovpak, J. 2016, "Russia to Reintroduce Forced Labor as Criminal Punishment," Voice of America, 13 October. Available from: https://www.voanews.com/a/russia-forced-labor/3549099.html. [30 November 2017].

79. Stulov, M. 2016, "Russian Justice System to Reintroduce Forced Labor in 2017," The Moscow Times, 4 October. Available from: https://themoscowtimes.com/news/russian-justice-system-to-reintroduce-forced-labor-in-2017-55589. [30 November 2017].

80. Президент России 2018, Федеральный закон от 23.04.2018 № 96-ФЗ: О внесении изменений в статью 53–1 Уголовного кодекса Российской Федерации и Уголовно-процессуальный кодекс Российской Федерации [President of Russia 2018, Federal Law No. 96-FZ of April 23, 2018 On Amending Article 53-1 of the Criminal Code of the Russian Federation and the Code of Criminal Procedure of the Russian Federation].Available from: http://kremlin.ru/acts/bank/42974. [2 May 2018].

81. Committee on the Elimination of Discrimination against Women 2015, "Concluding Observations on the Eighth Periodic Report of the Russian Federation United Nations Office of the High Commissioner." Available from: http://www.ohchr.org/EN/Issues/Slavery/SRSlavery/Pages/CountryVisits.aspx. [30 November 2017], OSCE Special Representative and Co-ordinator for Combating Trafficking in Human Beings, Madina Jarbussynova, 2017, "Report by OSCE Special Representative and Co-ordinator for Combating Trafficking in Human Beings," Madina Jarbussynova, following her official visit to the Russian Federation, 6-11 February 2017, Organization for Security and Co-operation in Europe. Available from: https://www.osce.org/cthb/107636. [9 April 2018].

Periodical and Internet Sources Bibliography

The following articles have been selected to supplement the diverse views presented in this chapter.

Priscilla Alvarez, "When Sex Trafficking Goes Unnoticed in America," *The Atlantic*, February 23, 2016. https://www. theatlantic.com/politics/archive/2016/02/how-sex-trafficking-goes-unnoticed-in-america/470166/.

Maria Fernanda Felix de la Luz, "Child Sex Tourism and Exploitation Are on the Rise: Companies Can Help Fight It," World Economic Forum, March 9, 2018. https://www.weforum.org/agenda/2018/03/changing-corporate-culture-can-help-fight-child-sex-tourism-heres-how/.

Anaya Pollard, "Sex Trafficking in Atlanta," Georgia State University, December 10, 2017. https://lds.gsu.edu/news/showcase/atlanta-studies/anaya-pollard/.

"Scale of the Issue," Stop the Trafik. https://www.stopthetraffik.org/about-human-trafficking/the-scale-of-human-trafficking/.

Tim Swarens, "Who Buys a Child for Sex? Otherwise Ordinary Men," IndyStar, January 30, 2018. https://www.indystar.com/story/opinion/columnists/tim-swarens/2018/01/30/exploited-human-trafficking-project-who-buys-child-sex-otherwise-ordinary-men/949512001/.

"What Is Human Trafficking?" US Department of Homeland Security. https://www.dhs.gov/blue-campaign/what-human-trafficking#.

"What Is Modern Slavery?," Anti Slavery International. https://www.antislavery.org/slavery-today/modern-slavery/.

"'Worst Human Traffickers' Include Russia, Belarus, Iran, Turkmenistan," Radio Free Europe, June 29, 2018. https://www.rferl.org/a/russia-belarus-iran-turkmenistan-human-traffickers-report/29326302.html.

GLOBALVIEWPOINTS

CHAPTER 2

Causes and Effects of Human Trafficking

Vulnerable Groups Are Especially Targeted for Human Trafficking

Heidi Box

In the following excerpted viewpoint Heidi Box offers a look at populations vulnerable to being trafficked worldwide, which most often includes women, children, political and ethnic minorities, the poor, and LGBTQ persons. Often, traffickers play on the individual's desire for valid employment or a chance for a more prosperous future, making this a cruel form of exploitation. Victims may lack education or sophistication, or they might come from rural areas from which they have rarely traveled. Heidi Box is a program assistant with the Colorado Attorney General's Office. She holds an MA in International Human Rights from the University of Denver, where she was an outreach coordinator and Research Associate with the Human Trafficking Clinic.

As you read, consider the following questions:

1. What are some common characteristics of those populations vulnerable to being exploited in human trafficking?
2. What role does gender play in populations prone to being exploited? What about the desire to be prosperous among those living in poverty?
3. What role does classic discrimination play among those most likely to be forced into human trafficking?

"Human Trafficking and Minorities: Vulnerability Compounded by Discrimination," by Heidi Box, University of Denver. Reprinted by permission.

Human trafficking is an extreme human rights violation that impacts all populations across the globe and is characterized by force, fraud, and coercion intended for exploitation (Palermo Protocol 2000). Currently, human trafficking research is particularly limited by non-standard terminology and a clandestine research population. While estimates of the number of trafficked persons vary widely and are notoriously unsubstantiated, we can still arrive at some conclusions regarding the overall number of trafficked persons. One low estimate suggests that in 2005, at least 2.4 million people had been trafficked into forced labor situations and approximately 12.3 million people were victims of forced labor (International Labour Organization 2005). In addition to compiling comprehensive data on the number of trafficked persons, researchers and policymakers must identify who is trafficked. Basic quantitative data on the raw numbers of trafficked persons is not enough; qualitative data is also required in order to combat this human rights violation. That is, what are the characteristics of trafficked persons; what do they have in common; and do those commonalities contribute to exploitation?

Research indicates that trafficked persons are typically poor, have few job prospects, limited access to education and may come from rural areas, depending on the country of origin (Omelaniuk 2005). As a result of these disadvantages, they are often compelled to migrate within or outside of the country for better economic opportunities (Laczko and Danailova-Trainor 2009). Thus, trafficked persons may willingly travel with an "employer" based on the promise of work as a waitress, farm worker, domestic worker, or in other industries. However, upon arriving at their destination, they may be refused wages or may be forced into another job entirely. In other cases, the individuals received an advance on their salary and are then told they must work for free to repay this debt, which is commonly known as debt bondage (Bedoya et al. 2009). Another common scenario is that of children sold by their parents, or of individuals (primarily women and girls) who were kidnapped or tricked by a boyfriend or family member, then sold to traffickers (e.g., Simkhada 2008). One of the underlying themes running through each of these scenarios is the desire for economic prosperity. Although existing research easily identifies the vital role of economics in human trafficking, it has failed to probe the complex relationship between poverty, discrimination, and other socio-cultural factors such as minority status. Consequently, there is a distinct lack of research relating to traditionally disadvantaged groups and systemic discrimination within the body of human trafficking literature.

One potentially significant, but often overlooked, criterion in anti-trafficking research is minority group membership. Although there is no internationally recognized definition of minorities (Office of the High Commissioner for Human Rights (OHCHR) 2008), the United Nations (UN) commonly identifies them as "persons belonging to national or ethnic, religious and linguistic minorities" (United Nations 1992). Alternatively, a definition created in 1977 by the Special Rapporteur of the UN Sub-Commission on the Prevention of Discrimination and Protection of Minorities, provides a clearer picture of what traditionally constitutes the term "minority:"

> A group numerically inferior to the rest of the population, in a non-dominant position [...] possessing distinct ethnic, religious or linguistic characteristics and showing a sense of solidarity aimed at preserving those characteristics (OHCHR 2008).

Although minority status is often tied to numerical inferiority, population size is not always a factor; indeed, majority members may experience systemic discrimination based on characteristics such as ethnicity, religion, and gender. Minority status and experience is also contextual based on location, with gender being the quintessential example. Gender affects women to varying degrees based on the country they live in, and in some cases women may suffer discrimination similar to that experienced by minorities. Thus, the historical definition of "minority" does not adequately reflect reality and limits the way we approach the trafficking of minorities. By broadening the term to encompass any group that

Human Trafficking in Black and White

The link between domestic sex trafficking and racial discrimination—while undeniable, is not immediately clear. What is clear; however, is that the demography of domestic sex trafficking is very different from the racial make up of the United States. In a recent report by the Office of Victims of Crime, of the confirmed sex trafficking victims, 40.4 percent of victims were African-American. This is almost four times higher than the percentage of African-Americans living in the United States, which the US Census Bureau currently lists as 13.1 percent of the total population. The FBI claims an even more surprising statistic for arrests under the age of 18, black children make up 55 % of all prostitution-related arrests in the United States.

White / Caucasian women and girls represent the second highest number of sex trafficking victims as 25.6 percent. This number is drastically lower than the current amount of White / Caucasian people in the United States, which as the majority ethnic group, makes up 75.1 percent of the country's total population. According to the report by the Office of Victims of Crime, women and girls who are African-American or White/Caucasian are more likely to become victims of sex trafficking than any other ethnic group in the United States. But why are African-American victims overrepresented and White/Caucasian victims underrepresented in sex trafficking?

Some argue that it is simple economics that causes racial disparities in trafficking—the demand for one race is higher than the demand for another. That could possibly explain why the percent of Asian American sex trafficking victims matches within one percent the racial makeup in the United States (four and five percent respectfully). Many traffickers are also savvy businessmen who are just trying to keep people that were marketable. In a recent Urban Institute study that looked at the economics of human trafficking, of the traffickers interviewed, the majority overwhelming believed that trafficking white women would make them more money but trafficking black women would land them less jail time if caught. Most of the traffickers interviewed had trafficked women and girls of different races since having a variety of products to sell was good for business.

"Human Trafficking: Not All Black or White," by Michelle Lillie, humantraffickingsearch, 2014.

suffers discrimination or marginalization, we enhance our ability to identify persons susceptible to trafficking.

The United Nations Declaration on the Rights of Persons Belonging to National or Ethnic, Religious and Linguistic Minorities focuses on protecting minority groups' culture and identity, but glosses over the myriad disadvantages that minorities face by virtue of group marginalization. Most commonly, minorities tend to be economically and politically disadvantaged, which leads to further inequalities, such as a lack of education (McDougall 2006). Minorities are disproportionately affected by poverty, thus, they may be more likely to migrate for better economic opportunities (Omelaniuk 2005). If we accept that susceptibility to trafficking is impacted and increased by powerful "push factors" like poverty, disenfranchisement, lack of education, and so on, then it follows that minority populations are likely to be prime targets for human traffickers. Although membership in a minority group may not be the primary reason for exploitation, it may increase vulnerability to trafficking. For example, indigenous peoples in Peru, Bolivia, and Paraguay are discriminated against in the work force and this prejudice is cited as the primary reason for income disparity between indigenous and non-indigenous peoples (Bedoya et al. 2009, 37). Furthermore, indigenous populations have historically experienced debt bondage in all three of these countries (Bedoya et al. 2009, 37.) This suggests that these marginalized groups are likely exploited by nonminority members after systemic inequality severely limits their job prospects. Essentially, poverty is compounded by discrimination. The Roma, a minority group concentrated in Europe, is subjected to virulent bigotry and studies indicate that they are at an increased risk of being trafficked within Albania, Romania, and Bulgaria (Omelaniuk 2005, 5).

Although evidence within the extant literature is suggestive of a link between disadvantaged populations and susceptibility to trafficking, this correlation has been insufficiently investigated. Indeed, it is surprising how little research has been done to explore human trafficking through the lens of minority discrimination.

Before policymakers can produce sustainable prevention and development policies, research must identify the strongest indicators of trafficking experienced by marginalized groups. This includes expanding the current ideology on minority groups in order to encompass the endemic bias and the resulting consequences they experience. We are likely to find that as a result of systemic inequality born of discrimination, minorities are at an increased risk of being trafficked and therefore minority group membership should be considered a risk factor for trafficking. Our understanding of each nuance of trafficked persons is vital if we intend to stem the flow of human trafficking.

The Internet Has Made Sex Trafficking a Worldwide Business

Fair Observer

In the following viewpoint authors from Fair Observer concentrate on the growing business of internet sex trafficking and how the ability to post anonymously online has exacerbated the problem of all sex trafficking, but child sexual exploitation in particular. The authors go on to discuss new legislation designed to combat trafficking in persons on the internet by holding companies liable for knowingly allowing the posting of illegal sex ads, and ways in which organizations can work together to eradicate the demand for human sex trafficking. Fair Observer is a not-for-profit media organization that publishes a crowdsourced multimedia journal that aims to educate and inform a global audience.

As you read, consider the following questions:

1. What is Backpage? How is it implicated in human trafficking crimes perpetrated on the internet?
2. What keywords or "flag" words are indicative of child sexual trafficking online?
3. When was FOSTA established and what does it hope to enact?

The internet has enabled sex trafficking to become the fastest growing criminal enterprise in the world, worth a staggering

"Interrupting the Vicious Cycle of Online Sex Trafficking," Fair Observer, August 3, 2018. Reprinted by permission.

$99 billion a year. This expansion correlates directly with the increasing use of digital platforms to sell people online, because like any other "successful" business, sex traffickers rely on marketing and communication tools to ensure a steady cycle of demand and supply.

Tragically, this industry boom is being fueled by an astronomical growth in child sex trafficking. Between 2010 and 2015, the National Center for Missing and Exploited Children's CyberTipline received an 846% increase in the number of suspected cases reported, and the US Department of Justice has said that more than half of sex-trafficking victims are 17 years old or younger.

"Adult" sections on mainstream classified websites normalize easy, anonymous ways for traffickers and pimps to recruit, market and deliver women and children as commodities for sexual exploitation. Posting an online ad is quick, cheap and simple, and victims can be repeatedly bought and sold for large sums of money at relatively low risk. Traffickers are able to advertise in multiple locations, test out new markets, locate customers and transport victims to meet buyers while avoiding detection by authorities.

Meanwhile, the transitory nature of online sex trafficking makes it harder for law enforcement to locate victims, pimps and buyers; identify essential witnesses and evidence; and share information and intelligence across jurisdictions.

FOSTA

In April, Congress passed FOSTA, a groundbreaking law that interrupts this cycle of abuse by holding internet companies accountable when they knowingly facilitate sex trafficking. An abbreviation for Allow States and Victims to Fight Online Sex Trafficking Act of 2017, FOSTA shrinks the online commercial sex market and opens up legal avenues for prosecutors and victims to take steps against social networks, websites and online advertisers that have failed to act sufficiently against users who post exploitative content.

However, not everyone is happy with FOSTA. Some have raised concerns that it will force online platforms to police their users' speech. There's even a lawsuit pending against the legislation. The plaintiffs, represented by the Electronic Frontier Foundation (EFF), a nonprofit that is funded in part by Google, call FOSTA an "unconstitutional Internet censorship law."

FOSTA is a very narrowly tailored law that specifically holds anyone who knowingly facilitates and supports sex trafficking online liable. It doesn't cast a wide net over all internet activity—that kind of approach would be impossible. Industry giants like Oracle, IBM, Disney, 20th Century Fox and Hewlett Packard backed the bill because they realize technology can be used for good and bad and we shouldn't leave it undefended against criminals.

Sheryl Sandberg, Facebook's chief operating officer, supported FOSTA saying, "We all have a responsibility to do our part to fight this," and that we should "allow responsible companies to continue fighting sex trafficking while giving victims the chance to seek justice against companies that knowingly facilitate such abhorrent acts." Others have said that without sites like Backpage. com, women who choose to be in prostitution have fewer tools to screen potential "johns" and, as a result, are left vulnerable. But FOSTA does not target the adult services sector nor individuals—it explicitly targets tech companies.

Backpage was involved in 73% of all child trafficking cases reported to the National Center for Missing and Exploited Children (excluding reports made by Backpage itself). Before FOSTA, victims who were trafficked via the website were repeatedly prevented from getting justice through the courts—even in cases when Backpage knew of or participated in posting advertisements for sex from minors.

What survivors and activists knew to be true for years was finally confirmed by federal investigators when Backpage CEO Carl Ferrer admitted the website went so far as to assist advertisers in wording their ads so they didn't overtly declare that sex with minors was for sale. Flagged keywords associated with trafficking—such as "Lolita," "rape," amber alert" and "teenage"—were deleted to conceal the true nature of the ads before they were published online.

The site, which was finally shut down in April 2018, may have been described as a "tool" for some but, in reality, it was overwhelmingly being used as a platform for commercial sexual exploitation—earning around $7 per ad. A Senate report found that around 93% of Backpage.com's revenue—estimated at $150 million in 2016—was from "adult services" ads.

Ending Demand

While FOSTA is a monumental law, it alone will not end the exploitation of women and girls in the United States. We have to address this cycle of abuse at the beginning—and that means ending demand.

Legal rights organization Equality Now is working alongside survivors of commercial sexual exploitation, women and children's rights organizations, policymakers and law enforcement officials to tackle the root causes of sex trafficking. This involves criminalizing those who exploit people for profit, including sex buyers, traffickers, pimps and brothel-keepers, and decriminalizing people in prostitution, including victims of trafficking, and providing them with much needed support services.

If we are going to make a dent in triple-digit percentage increases, we have to follow the money and hold those at the helm accountable. This is what FOSTA was made for.

July 30 marks World Day against Trafficking in Persons. Stand up for victims of online sex trafficking and together we can ensure the internet is no longer a tool for exploitation.

Human Trafficking Is Not Limited to Specific Countries or Regions

The Advocates for Human Rights

In the following viewpoint, taken from their educational resource materials on www.stopvaw.org, authors from The Advocates for Human Rights outline how trafficking affects all regions and the majority of countries in the world. Despite the clandestine and global nature of trafficking, certain common patterns emerge, such as trafficking flows from rural to urban areas within countries, and from less developed to more developed countries within regions. Based in Minneapolis, Minnesota, The Advocates for Human Rights, a 501(c) (3) organization, creates and maintains lasting, comprehensive, and holistic change on a local, national, and global scale. Their mission is to implement international human rights standards, to promote civil society and reinforce the rule of law.

As you read, consider the following questions:

1. How does the relationship between human trafficking origin, transit and destination countries create a worldwide problem?
2. What role does a disparity in wealth across nations play in the propagation of human trafficking?
3. Does domestic trafficking in persons qualitatively differ from trafficking people across international borders?

Trafficking in persons is not limited to specific countries or regions. According to the International Organization for Migration (IOM), human trafficking victims representing 169 different nationalities were identified in 172 countries worldwide.[1] Between 2010 and 2012, UN Office on Drugs and Crime also identified approximately 510 distinct human trafficking flows.[2] Although trafficking occurs worldwide, trafficking patterns and volumes may vary in different parts of the world.

Organizations that study trafficking patterns tend to classify countries as source or origin countries, transit countries or destination countries. However, this classification system can be misleading because many countries fall under each of these categories at some point.[3] Additionally, the UNODC has pointed out that trafficking flows are dominated less by clear geographic boundaries than by relative pockets of economic disparity, with victims flowing from poorer to richer areas within countries, regions or across the globe.[4]

In simple terms, a source or origin country is a country where traffickers commonly find and recruit women and girls for their operations. Once traffickers have recruited an individual, that person is moved through intermediary or transit countries, sometimes for extended periods during which the women may be forced into labor or the sex trade. Transit countries are chosen for the geographical location and are usually characterized by weak border controls, proximity to destination countries, corruption of immigration officials, or affiliation with organized crime groups that are involved in trafficking. In general, "organized criminals will try to push people over any border that is easiest for them to cross."[5] Destination countries are the last link in the human trafficking chain. These countries receive trafficking victims and are generally more economically prosperous than origin countries. Destination countries can support a large commercial sex industry or a forced labor industry, the modern equivalent of slavery. The financial return to traffickers per victim is also highest in richer countries.

Additionally, victims are most commonly trafficked within their home country or region of origin.[6] For example, in North Africa, over 80% of detected trafficking victims were trafficked domestically.[7] Further, in Eastern Europe and Central Asia, 100% of detected trafficking victims were trafficked within the same subregion, a statistic closely followed by South Asia (99%), Sub-Saharan Africa (99%), East Asia and the Pacific (97%), and South America (93%).[8]

Trafficking flows share certain similar traits no matter where they are found in the world. Certain dimensions of development in a given country have a direct effect on the likelihood of human trafficking within that country's borders. For example, poverty is one of the prime risk factors associated with human trafficking. When combined with other risk factors such as limited economic or educational opportunity, poor governance, weakened rule of law in post-conflict countries, and natural disaster, the conditions in a country become ripe for the exploitative practices of human traffickers. International destinations for trafficking most often include well-developed, wealthy and industrialized areas of the world. As stated by the UNODC in 2014,

> The 'global north' attracts victims from all over the world. Traffickers in poorer countries have an economic interest of moving victims there—to Western Europe, North America or the Middle East—while there is little to gain from moving victims in the opposite direction. In addition to economic factors, there are also other conditions that have an impact on the directions of trafficking flows. These include issues related to job markets, migration policy, regulation, prostitution policy, legal context and law enforcement and border control efficiency … [T]o traffic victims internationally is complicated and may involve significant risks … Relatively few traffickers are able to organize themselves well enough to conduct effective transregional trafficking activities.[9]

Analyzing and tracking human trafficking flows or routes is a difficult task given the still hidden nature of the crime and because traffickers regularly shift routes to avoid detection. In its 2016 Global Trafficking report, the UNODC noted that, "the available data is insufficient to delineate trafficking routes."[10] However, some work has been done to identify general flows, and the UNODC includes maps of major trafficking flows in its 2014 Global Report.

As noted by one commentator in the *European Journal of Criminology*, "[t]he lack of certainty about the legal responsibilities of origin, transit and destination countries helps traffickers continue to operate with impunity."[12] For this reason, it is vital that origin, transit and destination countries cooperate and develop joint strategies to combat trafficking. According to the US Department of State, "[d]estination countries must work with transit and source countries to stem the flow of trafficking; source countries must work not only to prevent trafficking, but to help with the reintegration of trafficking victims back into their home societies."[13]

Notes

1. United Nations Office on Drugs and Crime, "Global Report on Trafficking in Persons" 47 (2018) [hereinafter 2018 Global Report].
2. United Nations Office on Drugs and Crime, "Global Report on Trafficking in Persons" 5 (2014) [hereinafter 2014 Global Report].
3. United Nations Office on Drugs and Crime, "Global Report on Trafficking in Persons" 40 (2016) [hereinafter 2016 Global Report].
4. UNODC, 2018 Global Report 9.
5. Vesna Nikolić-Ristanović, et al., Organization for Security and Co-Operation in Europe, "Trafficking in People in Serbia" 161 (2004).
6. UNODC, 2018 Global Report 9, 23.
7. Id.at 87.
8. Id. at 9.
9. UNODC, 2014 Global Report 48.
10. UNODC, 2016 Global Report 40.
12. Benjamin Perrin, "Just Passing Through? International Legal Obligations and Policies of Transit Countries in Combating Trafficking in Persons," 7 *European J. Criminology* 11, 15 (2010) (citing M.A. Clark, Trafficking in Persons: An Issue of Human Security, 4 J. Human Development 247 (2003).
13. US Department of State, "Victims of Trafficking and Violence Protection Act of 2000: Trafficking in Persons Report" 5 (2002).

In the United Kingdom, a Portrait of Modern-Day Slavery

Gary Craig, Aline Gaus, Mick Wilkinson, Klara Skrivankova, and Aidan McQuade

In the following viewpoint, Gary Craig, Aline Gaus, Mick Wilkinson, Klara Skrivankova and Aidan McQuade offer a snapshot of human trafficking and modern-day slavery in the United Kingdom. The year 2007 marked a special date in that country, as it was the 200th anniversary of legislation officially abolishing slavery, and even though this report is by the time of this publishing nearly 15 years old, it still maintains relevance today, as modern-day slavery has only increased in volume all over the world in the past few years. The authors are affiliated with the Wilberforce Institute for the study of Slavery and Emancipation (WISE) at the University of Hull and Anti-Slavery International. The study was undertaken by a review of published literature and unpublished policy papers provided by service delivery agencies, a review of websites across the world (particularly in Western Europe), and interviews with key actors.

"Modern Slavery in the United Kingdom," by Gary Craig, Aline Gaus, Mick Wilkinson, Klara Skrivankova and Aidan McQuade, Joseph Rowntree Foundation, February 26, 2007. Reprinted by permission.

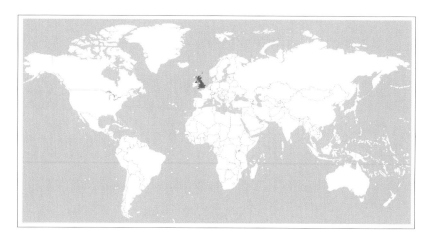

As you read, consider the following questions:

1. What are some key elements of modern-day slavery that make it so pernicious according to this viewpoint?
2. How does this viewpoint's premise differ in substance from the one in Chapter One that called for a change of terms and definitions regarding modern day slavery?
3. What ethnic groups or other groups have been especially affected by human trafficking in the United Kingdom?

2007 marks the 200th anniversary of the UK legislation abolishing the slave trade. Many people are unaware, however, that slavery continues to exist in the modern world and that forms of slavery are common within the UK. A joint research team, from the University of Hull and Anti-Slavery International, has been exploring the contours of modern slavery in the UK. It found:

- Modern slavery exists in the UK in various forms. All exhibit the common elements of the exploitative relationship which have always constituted slavery: severe economic exploitation; the absence of a framework of human rights; and control of one person over another by the prospect or reality of violence. Coercion distinguishes slavery from poor working conditions.

- It is, however, very difficult to compile precise statistics about the extent of slavery in the UK and official figures are widely recognised to be substantial underestimates. Slavery in the UK often comes to light only when a crisis occurs.

- Trafficking into the UK for sexual or domestic labour involves hundreds or even thousands of women and children. Some children, in particular those from African countries, are trafficked through the UK to other countries.

- Some forms—such as child labour—have existed for years but are increasingly constrained by international conventions to protect the rights of children. Although child labour is prohibited in the UK, there is a connection with the UK through the conditions under which sportswear and clothing, or commodities such as tea or cocoa, are produced.

- Some UK-based companies, knowingly or not, rely on people working in slavery to produce goods which they sell: complex sub-contracting and supply chains, managed by agents elsewhere, often obscure this involvement.

- The UK has tended to address trafficking as an issue of migration control rather than one of human rights.

- Most trafficked people enter the UK legally but become subject to forced labour through a mix of enforced debt, intimidation, the removal of documents and an inadequate understanding of their rights. Statutory agency personnel are often unsure how to assist trafficked migrant workers and keep few or no records as to their subsequent well-being.

- Slavery in contemporary Britain cannot be seen in isolation. Most of those working as slaves in the UK have come from elsewhere, often legally. Slavery is an international issue.

Background

With the growth of globalisation and migration, it has become clear that modern forms of slavery are growing in the UK. This study attempts to map its extent and nature, reviewing the evidence on key areas of slavery in the UK, particularly forced labour, debt bondage, sexual slavery, and child trafficking and labour.

What Is Slavery?

There is considerable confusion about the nature and boundaries of slavery. Definitions are therefore important.

Defining Slavery

There are three essential elements of the exploitative relationship which constitute slavery:

- severe economic exploitation;

- the lack of a human rights framework; and

- control of one person over another by the prospect or reality of violence. Many relationships of enslavement do not involve actual physical violence but the nature of the relationship— appalling working and housing conditions, the withdrawal of passports or ID documents, deceit and abuse of power, the use of physical intimidation—renders the possibility of flight remote. There is much evidence that those who do protest about such conditions may be beaten, abused, raped, deported or even killed.

Slavery and Poor Working Conditions

It is important to distinguish poor—or even appalling—working conditions from slavery. Coercion is the key distinction: the enslaved person has no real alternative but to submit to the abusive relationship. Abuse refers to the treatment of one person by another specific person and is distinct from being forced into dangerous or difficult work by economic circumstances or other impersonal forces.

The Polish Workers

A group of Polish people came to work in the UK. They had expected to go to Southampton but were brought to Exeter to pack chickens for a major supermarket. Arriving late at night, they waited outside a house whilst inside frightened-looking Afghans threw their own things into bin bags before being driven away. The Poles spoke no English, had no money and didn't know who they were working for. They were not employed directly by the factory supplying the supermarket but subcontracted in a complex supply chain through labour agencies.

They were taken by van to a 2-10pm shift. There was no furniture in the house, but there were mountains of rubbish, piles of syringes, soiled mattresses on the floor and a terrible smell. Twenty people slept there, three and four to a small room. They were threatened with eviction and loss of two weeks' wages by their gangmasters if they told anyone about their conditions. They were also told to be very quiet and not go out in groups or the police would come. They felt intimidated.

They had been recruited in Poland by an English labour agency. The agency had promised the minimum wage (then £4.50ph), good accommodation for £25 per person per week, and lots of overtime. They received neither work nor wages in their first week. Contracts they signed were made without translation. Although they were sleeping on the floor in the kitchen and sitting-room (and the legal maximum rent for those on the minimum wage is under £25), they were told they must pay rent of £40 each. This was deducted weekly from their pay.

Several were given the same National Insurance number. They had tax deducted at a high emergency rate. The Tax Office said it had not yet received payments for them. After deductions, they were getting just £115 a week for 40 hours (£2.88ph). Another £15 disappeared without explanation. Most had not registered with

Debt Bondage and Bonded Labor

We do not stop even if we are ill—what if our debt is increasing? So we don't dare to stop.

[Other workers] tried to leave, but two got caught. They locked them up and started beating them. They told the workers, "if you want to go from here, you must pay 60,000, that is your debt." —Puspal, former brick kiln worker in Punjab, India.

Puspal is one of millions of victims of bonded labour across the world. Also known as debt bondage or debt slavery, it is the most common form of modern slavery. Despite this, it's the least known.

Debt bondage occurs when a person is forced to work to pay off a debt. They are tricked into working for little or no pay, with no control over their debt.

Most or all of the money they earn goes to pay off their loan. The value of their work invariably becomes greater than the original sum of money borrowed.

Puspal managed to leave thanks to the great support her family received from our project partners, but usually that it is extremely difficult.

the Home Office because they could not afford the £50 required, but this made them vulnerable to deportation. The workers finally managed to escape after a local trades union became aware of them. Source: Lawrence, F. "Special Investigation. Polish Workers Lost in a Strange Land Find Work in the UK Does Not Pay," *The Guardian,* 11 January 2005.

Trafficking and Smuggling
The UN definition of trafficking for forced labour and other forms of slavery concerns the recruitment, transportation, transfer, harbouring or receipt of people, by means of the threat or use of force or other forms of coercion, in order to achieve control over another person.

People bonded by debt face coercion, violence and intimidation if they try to leave.

Bonded labour has existed for hundreds of years. Debt bondage was used to trap indentured labourers into working on plantations in Africa, the Caribbean and South-East Asia, following the abolition of the Transatlantic Slave Trade.

Bonded labour is most widespread in South Asian countries such as India and Pakistan. Often entire families have to work to pay off the debt taken by one of its members. Sometimes, the debt can be passed down the generations and children can be held in debt bondage because of a loan their parents had taken decades ago.

In South Asia it still flourishes in agriculture, brick kilns, mills, mines and factories. Anti-Slavery International works in India where hundreds of thousands of men, women and children are forced to work as bonded labourers in brick kilns and agriculture, often suffering extreme exploitation and abuse.

Debt bondage in a wider sense is spread much beyond South Asia and is an element of many other forms of slavery such as forced labour and trafficking. People borrow money to pay their traffickers for a promised job abroad. Once at their destination their passports are taken away and they cannot leave until they pay off the debts they owe to their traffickers.

"What Is Bonded Labour?" Anti-Slavery International.

In practice, trafficking and smuggling overlap substantially but there are important distinctions:

- Smuggling involves explicit consent to be taken illegally across national borders. The relationship between smuggler and migrant typically ends when the destination is reached.

- Trafficking involves ongoing exploitation: even if the person has at some stage consented, this is meaningless because of the deception and coercion involved. Trafficking occurs within as well as across national borders.

How Extensive Is Slavery?

It is very difficult to compile precise statistics about the extent of slavery in the UK.

Official agencies, including the police and the Home Office, acknowledge that there are no reliable estimates for the number of trafficked people in the UK. The Solicitor General has suggested that more than 1,000 women were trafficked into the UK for sexual purposes (mainly from Eastern and Central Europe): this is recognised as a substantial underestimate. Others are trafficked for domestic labour. Perhaps thousands of young people have been trafficked through the UK to work as sex slaves elsewhere in Europe or as domestic labour in the UK. There are at least 5,000 child sex workers in the UK, most trafficked into the country. Many people trafficked into this country enter legally but then find themselves compelled to work as sexual or domestic slaves.

There are approximately 1.4 million registered foreign workers in the UK; estimates of the number of illegal workers range from about 300,000 to 800,000. Illegal workers are not necessarily slaves, and those working in slavery may have entered the UK either legally or illegally. The case studies show how even relatively skilled workers entering the country legally may find themselves working in enslaved conditions.

Worldwide, it is estimated that more than 12 million people may be working as slaves. These include at least 360,000 in industrialised countries, of whom at least 270,000 have been trafficked into forced labour. Of these, approximately 43 per cent are trafficked into sexual exploitation, approximately 32 per cent into labour exploitation and about 25 per cent are exploited for a mix of sexual and labour reasons.

The ILO estimates that the worldwide traffic in human beings is worth at least US$32 billion annually, just under half coming from traffic to industrialised countries. The ILO and UNICEF suggest that in 2004, 218 million children were trapped in child labour worldwide. Of these, by 2006, some 171 million were engaged in "hazardous work" including in factories, mines and agriculture. In

2003, an estimated 3-4.5 million people were living in the European Union without legal papers, with an estimated 400,000 people a year being trafficked into member states.

Slavery in the UK: Some Issues

Where Are They Working?

Migrant workers—whether illegal migrants or legal migrants working illegally—are most at risk of slavery or slavery-like working conditions. They are found in a wide variety of employment, including domestic work, construction, agriculture and food-related occupations, sexual activity, and many marginal economic activities. Many come expecting certain kinds of work but end up doing others: for example, women from the Baltic States were purposely trafficked for illicit activities such as shoplifting (though they had not been told this when recruited).

Who Controls Them?

UK enforcement agencies estimate there may be as many as 10,000 gangmasters operating across the various industrial sectors. Most employ migrant labour in agriculture, food processing and packing, construction, catering, leisure, hotels, cleaning, textiles, and social and health care. Many operate legally. However, thousands of migrant workers working apparently legally do so under levels of exploitation which meet the international legal definition of "forced labour," one form of slavery.

A Latvian Woman

In her early 20s, she arrived in London on her own initiative, leaving her young children behind. She was recruited by an employment agency at £100 fee. They moved her to Hull, taking her passport, ostensibly to send to the Home Office for registration. After four months she hadn't received her passport back (it had not been sent off). This later affected her benefit status and, without it, she felt unable to leave the agency. She regularly worked 16-hour shifts in factories, under threat of losing her job and accommodation if she refused. Overtime was never paid. She was transported to work double shifts in Barnsley, sleeping in a car between shifts. Spurious deductions for "administration charges" and "transport costs" were the norm and there was evidence of systematic theft through the deliberate miscalculation of wages. Sometimes migrants worked two shifts only to be paid for one. Her protestations were met with threats of dismissal. She was placed in a bedroom with two men she did not know. Her general mood was "Terrible. Having to live in a room with two men. You can't dress. You can't do anything." She didn't know where to go to for advice, her English wasn't strong and she had no friends. She described herself as "trapped." Source: Case study by research team.

How Has Government Responded?

There has been recent legislation and a Human Trafficking Centre has been established to co-ordinate responses. However, migration is such a controversial issue in the UK that the approach to trafficking has at times emphasised law enforcement at the expense of the protection needs of the victim. The UK has thus tended to address trafficking as an issue of migration control rather than one of human rights. Victims are often deported back to the original country from which they were trafficked: here they may be threatened, assaulted, retrafficked, or face humiliation from their families. Generally, the regulatory environment is complex and poorly resourced.

How Do They Get Here?

Most trafficked people enter the UK legally through regular migration routes and work visas. What then subjects them to forced labour is usually some mix of "debt bondage" (the requirement to pay back debts which, because of low or no wages and illegal deductions, they are never able to do), the removal of documents and an inadequate understanding of their rights. Statutory agency personnel dealing with trafficked migrant workers are often unsure how to assist them or who to refer them to and keep few, if any, records as to their subsequent well-being.

Are UK Companies Involved?

Some, possibly many, UK-based companies rely on supply chains which involve the use of slave labour both in the UK and abroad. The complex chains of subcontracting through a variety of labour agencies and networks, both in the UK and abroad, means many companies are unaware of or can deny knowledge of the conditions under which their goods are produced. Big brand fashion retailers and food and related retailers squeeze developing world suppliers and this pressure on prices, when passed down the supply chain, translates into exploitation of workers. Employers in developing countries find ways around corporate codes of ethical trading and UK-based corporations do not police them in any meaningful way.

Vietnamese Men

Two Vietnamese men in their twenties were promised a job at a hotel in the UK, paying £18,000 each to their agent in Vietnam for this arrangement. They came to the UK under the government's work permit scheme with a promise of receiving £4.95 per hour for their work. A representative from an agency supplying workers to major hotel chains met them at the airport and took their passports. They were put to work in a hotel. They worked for two months without receiving any pay, only food. They attempted to strike but, almost immediately, their families in Vietnam received threats. They approached the local Citizens' Advice Bureau via a Vietnamese-speaking person they met on the street. They are too frightened to approach the Vietnamese Embassy, but want to warn others. Source: Citizens Advice Journal.

Conclusion

The researchers conclude that the following measures are needed:

- National action complemented by international law and collaborative action.

- Policy and service responses which regard those in slavery as victims first and foremost.

- A more robust stance against the exploiters and proper resources for enforcement agencies. Since the 2004 Asylum and Immigration Act, there has yet to be a single prosecution brought for trafficking for labour exploitation.

- Training in awareness of how to identify slavery conditions. Local service providers—including local authorities and advice agencies, housing bodies, church groups and trades unions—are often those which slaves first contact.

- A public awareness campaign.

Periodical and Internet Sources Bibliography

The following articles have been selected to supplement the diverse views presented in this chapter.

Jessa Dillow Crisp, "'I Remember the Smells, the Sights, and the Taste of Slavery': Jessa Dillow Crisp Shares Her Story," Global Poverty Project, January 4, 2017. https://www.globalcitizen.org/en/content/jessa-dillow-crisp-i-remember-the-smells-the-sight/.

Micah Hartmann, "Causes and Effects of Human Trafficking," The Exodus Road, November 9, 2018. https://blog.theexodusroad.com/causes-effects-of-human-trafficking.

"A Human Trafficking Victim Shares Her Story," United States Department of Homeland Security, November 2, 2017.

Deidre McPhillips, "5 of the Worst Countries for Human Trafficking," *US News and World Report*, July 28, 2017. https://www.usnews.com/news/best-countries/slideshows/5-of-the-worst-countries-for-human-trafficking.

Bianca Jinete Mejia, "Source Countries in International Human Trafficking: A Time Series Analysis," Wartburg College. http://public.wartburg.edu/mpsurc/images/mejia.pdf.

National Human Trafficking Hotline, https://humantraffickinghotline.org

John Cotton Richmond, "The Root Cause of Human Trafficking Is Traffickers," The Human Trafficking Institute, January 31, 2017. https://www.traffickinginstitute.org/the-root-cause-of-trafficking-is-traffickers/.

"Trafficking Explained," European Commission. https://ec.europa.eu/anti-trafficking/citizens-corner/trafficking-explained_en.

Melissa Withers, "How US Citizens Become Human Trafficking Victims," *Psychology Today,* November 3, 2016. https://www.psychologytoday.com/us/blog/modern-day-slavery/201611/how-us-citizens-become-human-trafficking-victims.

CHAPTER 3

Types of Human Trafficking and Its Global Impact

Organ Trafficking Is a Gruesome and Lucrative Form of Global Human Trafficking

Christina Bain and Joseph Mari

In the following viewpoint Christina Bain and Joseph Mari discuss a form of human trafficking that doesn't get much attention in the popular press, that of illicit human organ harvesting and trafficking. This is a crime that hides in plain sight, with an estimated 10 percent of all organ transplants derived from illicit sources. The demand for organs such as kidneys, corneas, lungs, and hearts is very high and the supply is low, with irreparable harm caused to vulnerable populations targeted for the harvesting of these body parts, even if lives are not taken. The authors write from the point of view of monitoring large cash flows with the intent to purchase organs and how best to deter this activity. Christina Bain is director of the initiative on human trafficking and modern slavery, Babson College. Joseph Mari is a certified anti-money laundering specialist and senior manager of major investigations, Bank of Montreal.

"Organ Trafficking: The Unseen Form of Human Trafficking," by Christina Bain and Joseph Mari, under the advisory of Dr. Francis L. Delmonico, ACAMS Today, Association of Certified Anti-Money Laundering Specialists, June 26, 2018. Reprinted by permission.

As you read, consider the following questions:

1. Why might the crime of illicit organ trafficking be such a rarely discussed form of human trafficking?
2. What are ways in which organ trafficking may appear to be legitimate as far as the donor/recipient relationship?
3. What legitimate organizations and professionals can be left vulnerable to the exchange of cash via organ purchase if such money laundering is not detected?

Organ trafficking, a lucrative global illicit trade, is often a lesser discussed form of human trafficking among anti-human trafficking stakeholders due to its intricate and often stealth nature. Trafficking sex and/or labor are the more commonly thought of forms of human trafficking among public policy leaders and general awareness campaigns. However, organ trafficking holds a critical place with transnational organized crime groups due to high demand and relatively low rates of law enforcement.

Organ traffickers profit in the shadows, while their destructive medical footprint is the only thing that is felt. It leaves vulnerable populations, aka "donors," and first world beneficiaries, aka "recipients," open to severe exploitation and a lifetime of health consequences.

This form of illicit trade also leaves the private sector, in particular the financial industry, susceptible to being an unknowing conduit for its facilitation. Although, with the right training and raised awareness, financial institutions may play a pivotal role in unmasking organ traders by way of the financial trail they leave behind.

Low Supply, High Demand

When describing organ trafficking, there is often confusion as to how this crime can happen. Global Financial Integrity (GFI) estimates that 10 percent of all organ transplants including lungs, heart and liver, are done via trafficked organs.[1] However, the most prominent organs that are traded illicitly are kidneys, with the World Health Organization (WHO) estimating that 10,000 kidneys are traded on the black market worldwide annually, or more than one every hour.[2]

On their own, these numbers can be stark; however, when compared to average wait times for organs in developed countries, one can start to better understand the demand being diverted to black markets. In Canada, it is estimated that the average wait time for a kidney is 4 years with some waiting as long as 7 years.[3] In the US, the average wait time for a kidney is 3.6 years according to the National Kidney Foundation.[4] In the UK, wait times average 2 to 3 years but could be longer.[5]

Hiding in Plain Sight

Once obtained, trafficked organs can be transplanted to recipients in the most reputable of hospitals in major cities throughout the world but makeshift operating rooms in houses have often been the clandestine locations for such transplants.

Traffickers orchestrate the recruitment of the donor often from a place of vulnerability, and victims are not necessarily properly screened for their qualifications to be a healthy donor. Desperate patients in need of an organ may fall prey to a trafficker who could be posing as a "reputable" representative of an altruistic organ matching organization. Financial exploitation plays a key part in both sides of this scenario. In addition, organ traffickers could also be involved in other forms of human trafficking, such as sex and/or labor trafficking. Cases are emerging where an organ donor may have been a victim of sex trafficking and/or labor trafficking as well as a victim of organ trafficking, creating a multi-level equation of exploitation. The term "transplant tourism" is often utilized in describing this crime, as defined by the Declaration of Istanbul:

> … travel for transplantation that involves organ trafficking and/or transplant commercialism or if the resources (organs, professionals and transplant centers) devoted to providing transplants to patients from outside a country undermine

the country's ability to provide transplant services for its own population.[6]

Expanding the Human Trafficking Lexicon

How does organ trafficking fit within the broader definition of human trafficking? As stated in the Palermo Protocol of 2000, the basis for most national laws on human trafficking, organ trafficking is defined within the broader definition as:

> Trafficking in persons shall mean the recruitment, transportation, transfer, harbouring or receipt of persons, by means of the threat or use of force or other forms of coercion, of abduction, of fraud, of deception, of the abuse of power or of a position of vulnerability or of the giving or receiving of payments or benefits to achieve the consent of a person having control over another person, for the purpose of exploitation. Exploitation shall include, at a minimum, the exploitation of the prostitution of others or other forms of sexual exploitation, forced labour or services, slavery or practices similar to slavery, servitude or the removal of organs.[7]

In most countries, the buying and selling of organs is illegal (e.g., Iran is the only country in the world where buying and selling an organ is legal but this exception only applies to its citizens). Conversely, there are few laws that restrict an individual from leaving one's country to obtain an organ from someone abroad. In fact, there are many companies that cater to "transplant tourism" but purport to only match up recipients with donors who are willing.

It is difficult to know exactly how much transplant tourism generates annually worldwide but it is estimated that the illegal organ trade conservatively generates approximately $840 million to $1.7 billion annually, according to GFI.[8]

Unfortunately, even with estimated flow of funds crossing $1 billion annually, it is difficult for both law enforcement agents and anti-money laundering (AML) professionals to detect related financial activity. This is due to a myriad of factors such as a lack of domestic laws deterring citizens from travelling abroad, the transnational nature of the crime, and the savviness of the purveyors who know the laws related to organ trafficking well enough to circumvent them by way of shell companies and sanitized (legal) offerings via public websites.

Money Laundering Indicators

While it may be difficult for banks to detect financial transactions related to organ trafficking, it is not impossible as there are some indicators available. These red flags could include the following indicators and may be innocuous on their own but when combined, could present potentially suspicious behavior:

- Wire transfers to entities in high-risk jurisdictions with names that include a variation of medical. For example, "Medicus"

- Methods of payment such as wire payments, email money transfer, and bulk cash withdrawal (See Table for estimated organ pricing)

- Payments between charities and medical tourism sites

- Credit card payments to travel agencies, airlines or hotels, prior to movement of money and travel

- First-line banking staff indication of potentially ill customers moving large amounts of funds to numbered companies or charities prior to travel

- Medical tourism websites that offer transplant services abroad that recommend utilizing their own trusted domestic doctors prior to traveling

One thing to keep in mind is that while traveling abroad to obtain an organ may be legal in certain countries, associated financial transactions would still be considered reportable in many jurisdictions as the act of purchasing an organ may be illegal within their country of citizenship. This stance gives AML professionals an interesting perspective above and beyond that of law enforcement as they are in a position to offer up intelligence that law enforcement agencies may have no insight on, nor a requirement to.

Intelligence gathered by financial intelligence units (FIUs) within financial institutions associated with organ trafficking or transplant tourism can be further disseminated to international partners by national FIUs.

Estimated Organ Pricing in US Dollars

Body Part	Price
Corneas	from $30,000
Lungs	from $150,000
Heart	from $130,000
Liver	from $98,000
Kidneys	from $62,000

SOURCE: Bloody Harvest Matas & Kilgour

Project Protect Expands: Project Organ

As previously stated, reporting on transactions related to organ trafficking is no easy feat. This way of raising awareness may prove to be an equally effective tool in deterring organ trafficking while increasing investigative knowledge toward reporting transactions.

One example of how awareness is being raised, within the context of AML and organ trafficking, is through the Project Protect initiative in Canada, launched by AML guru, Peter Warrack, in 2016. While initially designed to address sex trafficking, Project Protect was expanded to cover organ trafficking at the request of Dr. Francis L. Delmonico, M.D., professor of surgery at Harvard Medical School in 2018. The expansion is now known as "Project Organ" and its goals are similar to that of the original project, as it seeks to raise awareness and increase reporting to Canada's national FIU, the Financial Transactions and Reports Analysis Centre of Canada.

Looking Forward

Countries like the US and Canada did not include organ trafficking as a form of human trafficking when adopting their national laws on human trafficking. However, in the US for example, some individual states like Massachusetts include organ trafficking within their state laws on human trafficking.

Since the Palermo Protocol, the public policy discourse of organ trafficking has been steadily gaining. In 2008, a group of key stakeholders in the global fight against organ trafficking convened to form the Declaration of Istanbul, which after Istanbul, created crucial new definitions around organ trafficking and transplant tourism, and developed promising practices to tackle the organ trade. Dr. Delmonico was one of the co-founders of the Declaration of Istanbul and consequently, the Declaration of Istanbul Custodian Group (DICG), an international body tasked with implementing the principles of the Declaration. He said the following:

> The DICG has been an effective group of international colleagues monitoring illegal practices by their awareness of patients who return to their home country for sophisticated medical care following an organ transplant. Notifying the responsible authorities has led to the arrest of organ traffickers in Israel, China, Pakistan, India, Costa Rica, Egypt, and the United States.

In addition, the Council of Europe has adopted a Convention Against Trafficking in Human Organs in 2014 which recently went into effect in January of 2018.[9] This is a critical development as the first legal mechanism with a more universally agreed upon definition of organ trafficking.

More recent events, such as the February 2017 Summit on Organ Trafficking hosted by the Pontifical Academy of Sciences in Vatican City, have also shed light on the state of the organ trade.

As of today, the extent of organ trafficking is still unknown as to the number of such transplants performed annually. Furthermore, the full integration of the issue within the human trafficking field as a whole is still lacking.

In order to effectively combat organ trafficking and also raise its visibility among other forms of transnational organized crimes, it is vital to engage in effective public-private partnerships. The private sector, including the financial industry, can be essential in this global fight.

Notes

1. "Transnational Crime and the Developing World," Global Financial Integrity, March 2017, http://www.gfintegrity.org/wp-content/uploads/2017/03/Transnational_Crime-final.pdf.
2. Denis Campbell and Nicola Davison, "Illegal Kidney Trade Booms as New Organ Is Sold Every Hour,'" *The Guardian*, May 27, 2012, https://www.theguardian.com/world/2012/may/27/kidney-trade-illegal-operations-who.
3. "Organ Donation," The Kidney Foundation of Canada, https://www.kidney.ca/organ-donation.
4. "Organ Donation and Transplantation Statistics," National Kidney Foundation, https://www.kidney.org/news/newsroom/factsheets/Organ-Donation-and-Transplantation-Stats.
5. "Waiting List," NHS, October 14, 2015, https://www.nhs.uk/conditions/kidney-transplant/waiting-list/.
6. "The History and Development of the Declaration of Istanbul," Declaration of Istanbul on Organ Trafficking and Transplant Tourism, https://www.declarationofistanbul.org/about-the-declaration/history-and-development.
7. "United Nations Convention Against Transnational Organized Crime and the Protocols Thereto," United Nations Office on Drugs and Crime, 2004, https://www.unodc.org/documents/treaties/UNTOC/Publications/TOC%20Convention/TOCebook-e.pdf.
8. "Transnational Crime and the Developing World," Global Financial Integrity, March 2017, http://www.gfintegrity.org/wp-content/uploads/2017/03/Transnational_Crime-final.pdf.
9. "Trafficking in Human Organs: Council of Europe Convention Enters into Force," Council of Europe, January 3, 2018, https://www.coe.int/en/web/cdpc/-/trafficking-in-human-organs-council-of-europe-convention-enters-into-force.

Illegal Adoption Is Not a Form of Human Trafficking

Amber Moffett

In the following viewpoint Amber Moffett argues that while intercountry illegal adoption has much in common with human trafficking, it is not the same thing and has been left out of laws designed to prohibit other forms of human trafficking. There are many reasons for this, the main reason being that an adopted child is not considered to be exploited, although an argument can be made that biological parents of intercountry adoptions are exposed to this kind of abuse. Amber Moffett is a researcher who served as Graduate Associate Director of the Human Trafficking Center.

As you read, consider the following questions:

1. Why doesn't the author consider illegal overseas or intercountry adoptions the same as cases of human trafficking? Does that absolve the participants of responsibility?
2. In what ways is illegal intercountry adoption similar to human trafficking according to this viewpoint? In what ways does it differ?
3. Who might be the target audience for this viewpoint? How could it benefit them to read it?

Why choose to adopt a child from another country? For many, it's the inability to have a child themselves. For others, it may be that they simply want to provide a child with the opportunity for a better life than what would be provided them in a third-world orphanage. But imagine you have adopted a child, only to find out later that this very child you have grown to love and cherish was actually kidnapped and sold into an adoption scheme. Though this isn't every intercountry adoption (ICA) story, it is the incredibly unfortunate story of many.

Parallels Between ICA and Human Trafficking

Several interesting parallels can be seen between ICA and human trafficking. Both increase in times of armed conflict or in post-conflict settings. We saw this happen in the final days of the Vietnam War when Operation Babylift was carried out. Rumors of what the approaching communists would do to children fathered by American soldiers were used to coerce mothers into relinquishing their children to Americans who would fly them back to the US to be adopted and given a "better life." Similarly, El Salvador saw children being sold into illegal adoption networks during their civil war ending in 1992.

Another major parallel is the difference in national wealth between countries of origin and countries of destination. Many of the primary sending countries for both ICA and human trafficking are poorer countries (Guatemala, areas of China, Sierra Leone, Venezuela), whereas the countries of destination are often much wealthier (United States, United Kingdom, Australia, etc.). In this way, it becomes apparent that poverty is a major driving factor of both activities. When each child adoption is able to bring in anywhere from $25,000-50,000 to the local economy, fraudulent adoption can become a very lucrative industry, particularly for those in low-income countries.

Furthermore, both flourish in areas in which corruption is rampant and regulation is either non-existent or unenforced. Kevin Bales found that governmental corruption was the biggest predictor of human trafficking in a country of origin. Work done within the Human Trafficking Center has also found similar results—that corruption is one of the primary driving forces in the existence of human trafficking within a country. Similarly, ICA is seen with tremendous prevalence within corrupt countries. Of the top ten sending countries for ICA between 2003 and 2010, all but one was found to be highly rated on corruption indices.

Legally Failing Children in Illegal Adoption

It may come as a surprise to many, but despite the similarities found, illegal ICA is not considered to be human trafficking. In order to be qualify as human trafficking, three criteria must be met—Act, Means, and Purpose. Illegal and fraudulent adoption only has the first two of these three required elements. Though there definitely can be individual instances found in which all three qualifications apply, generally the child is not considered to be exploited.

Getting this issue covered under the US human trafficking statutes has proven difficult. One reason for this is money. As previously stated, ICA brings in quite a profit for many adoption agencies in both the US and in sending countries. Another reason is how hard it can be for adoptive parents to face the reality of how they got their child. Many fear they might lose their children to the biological parents that never gave up hope and want the child back. Others simply aren't interested in facing the truth that they paid thousands of dollars to someone who may have played a role in the kidnapping of their adopted child. Because of these reasons, it's been difficult to garner enough support in the US to modify US law to include "children bought/taken for the purposes of adoption" in the legal definition for human trafficking.

Alternative Legal Recourse

This is not to say that there is no legal recourse for these types of unethical practices. Alternative international statutes can be helpful in deterring fraudulent practices in ICA. The Convention

Illegal Adoption in China

China has a thriving domestic black market in children, mostly involving buyers who want them as slave labour. Most of the children are bought or kidnapped by gangs who force them into pick-pocketing and other non-violent crime in China's eastern cities. The children might also end up in a prostitution network or illegal adoption. According to a study by the University of Iowa, in November 2005, Chinese authorities uncovered a baby trafficking ring involving six orphanages and babies primarily from the southern part of the country. It is unclear how the children were obtained, but defendants claim the babies were abandoned or kidnapped.

In 2011, Chinese authorities arrested 370 persons and saved 89 children from being sold. Because of the "one child policy," some Chinese parents abandoned their second child. Indeed, a family that has more than one child is fined and loses a lot of social benefits. [China ended the one-child policy in 2016 due to dwindling birth rates.] Unfortunately, abandon is a common practice. In the worst cases parents sell their second child to local officials who in turn, sell them to orphanages.

Another problem is kidnapping. Organisations estimate that about 60,000 children between the ages of 2 to 4 are kidnapped every year, often sold to orphanages and end up in American or European families. In 2006, 10,000 children were adopted from China, with 7,000 going to the United States. Adoptive parents usually pay around $15,000 to $20,000 to adopt a child. The big challenge for organisations is to know if adopted children were kidnapped or not. For some parents, it raised a nightmarish question: What if my child had been taken forcibly from their parents?

Though the Chinese Government believes that birth control limits are essential for China to control an increasing population that will soar over the next 20 years, probably peaking at around 1.5 billion, it is aware of the situation and is ready to tighten adoption rules to combat child trafficking. Therefore, only orphanages will be able to offer abandoned infants and children for adoption, and adults who adopt without official registration will not be recognized as legal guardians. According to Ji Gang, the director of the domestic adoption department of the China Centre for Children's Welfare and Adoption, forcing people to go through official adoption channels will reduce the demand for abducted children.

"Illegal Adoption," United Nations, March 25, 2019.

on the Rights of the Child may prove useful, stating that "as far as possible, the right to know and be cared for by his or her parents" is a right of every child. It could be argued that children illegally adopted have been denied this right. Furthermore, the Hague Convention on Protection of Children and Co-operation in Respect of Intercountry Adoption stipulates that "intercountry adoptions take place in the best interests of the child … and prevent the abduction, the sale of, or traffic in children." However, what is considered to be in the "best interests of the child" is subject to wide interpretation, and not all countries are signatories to this convention.

There also has been a compelling argument made for the birth mothers to be considered the victims of human trafficking in instances of illegal adoption, falling under all three criteria mentioned above (action, means and purpose). In some instances, birth mothers are recruited (the action) and forced, coerced, or deceived (the means), resulting in the acquisition of a child (exploitation of the woman, the purpose).

Conclusion

To be clear, this is not to say that all ICAs are the product of the unethical practices of those looking to make a profit. It is also not to say that ICAs should be discouraged or discontinued. However, due diligence needs to be paid on all levels. Local governments need to be held accountable in protecting parents and children against kidnapping and coercive practices used to make a profit. If we are to ensure that the rights of children are protected and that adoptions are, in fact, "in the best interest of the child," extreme caution and extensive vetting needs to be the name of the game.

In the Philippines, Bangladesh, South America, and North Korea, Stories of Modern-Day Slavery

Annie Kelly and Kate Hodal

In the following excerpted viewpoint, Annie Kelly and Kate Hodal relay several stories of people who have experienced human trafficking scenarios first hand and later escaped from those situations. The authors tell the story of Elvira, of the Philippines, who was first forced into domestic slavery in Qatar, and later in the United Kingdom; Ali from Bangladesh, who was exploited as a debt bondage worker in Singapore; Mario of Peru, who was in a forced labor agreement working in a gold mine; Young-soon of North Korea, who was imprisoned in a labor camp; and Nelson, from Brazil, whose entire family was trapped on a coffee farm and not paid for their labor. Annie Kelly is a human rights journalist and editor of the Guardian's *Modern-day Slavery in Focus series. Kate Hodal has served as the* Guardian's *Southeast Asia correspondent.*

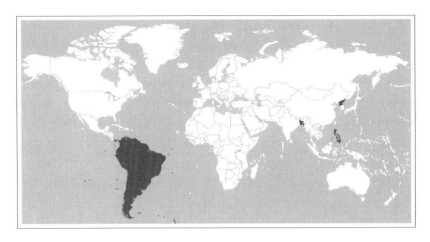

As you read, consider the following questions:

1. How do these personal stories of people trapped in slave-like conditions affect your individual worldview?
2. What do these various people have in common with each other?
3. Why do you think most forms of modern-day slavery slip under the legal radar with perpetrators rarely punished?

When Elvira arrived at Heathrow in 2014, she thought she had escaped the abuse she'd faced as a domestic worker in Qatar. Yet the exploitation the Filipino woman was about to suffer would surpass anything she experienced in the Middle East. The 50-year-old was taken to a luxury flat in Kensington, where her boss, the sister of her "madam" in Qatar, made her work 20 hours a day, allowing her only one piece of bread and no wages. She was trapped in a life of servitude, while metres away central London bustled with shoppers.

More than 200 years since it was abolished, slavery is thriving. The UN's International Labour Organisation estimates that 21 million people around the world are trapped in some form of modern slavery. In many cases, the physical shackles of the past have been replaced by less visible but equally effective forms of coercion and control: a worker on a factory line crippled by recruitment debts he or she cannot pay back; a man on a construction site in a foreign country without his passport or wages; a woman selling drugs on a roadside threatened with beatings and rape if she doesn't earn enough. Dig deep into the supply chain of the world's major commodities, and you'll find instances of slavery. From the food we eat to the phones we use and the clothes we wear, its influence is pervasive.

Record numbers of people are fleeing violence and poverty, and traffickers are ready to exploit them. The International Office for Migration believes 70% of migrants arriving in Europe by boat have been victims of human trafficking, organ trafficking or exploitation. In the UK, the government estimates there are 13,000 people trapped in slavery, working in hotels, care homes, nail bars and car washes, or locked in private houses that have been turned into brothels.

"As a business model, slavery is a no-brainer," says Siddharth Kara, an economist and director of human trafficking and modern slavery at Harvard's Kennedy school of government. "It's a low-cost, low-risk business that generates huge profits. To be two or three centuries on from the first efforts to eradicate slavery and still to have it permeating every corner of our economy is a damning indictment of our failure to tackle this highly lucrative criminal industry."

In London, Elvira managed to make a bold escape, waiting until her "employer" was taking a nap before running to a nearby church for sanctuary. She is still waiting for justice. Much exploitation goes unpunished and unrecognised: data from the US State Department shows that in 2016 there were only 9,071 convictions globally for forced labour and trafficking offences.

To get a picture of what slavery looks like today, we talked to people all over the world who have experienced it first-hand. Their stories, which show how quickly one can become trapped and exploited, give an insight into one of the biggest human rights challenges of our time.

Elvira, 50, Phillipines: Trafficked into Domestic Slavery in the UK

When my husband became very sick and couldn't work, I used an employment agency to find me work abroad. I was sent to Qatar, but the family were cheating me, paying me less than agreed in my contract and refusing to give me a day off. I called the agency in the Philippines for help, but they never answered. I had to send money back home to pay for food, school fees and medicine. I fought with my employer about my salary, but he would say: "Your contract is just a piece of paper."

A year passed. Finally, they said they'd let me go home if I went to work for one of their sisters, who lived in London. My employer flew with me, and when we reached Heathrow, the immigration officer just asked my employer what I'd be doing and let us through. The sister lived in a flat near Harrods. I had to work all the time, without a day off, and I slept on the floor by her bed. She'd shout at me, saying I was stupid or calling me a "dog" in Arabic. I was rarely allowed outside the house, and only with her. I was given just a piece of bread and cup of tea for the whole day. I became emaciated. I felt like a slave, like I was in prison. I wanted to run away, but they had my passport.

I had my phone, so I was able to get on Facebook, and a friend referred me to a federation of Filipino workers in London. One morning, after my employer went for a nap, I grabbed my phone, found the keys to the door and ran. I hid inside a nearby church and phoned the federation. I hope to get justice and go home soon.

[…]

Ali, 24, Bangladesh: Trapped in Debt Bondage Constructing Tower Blocks in Singapore

This is my first time in Singapore, and it cost me S$18,000 (£10,175) to get here. I was told I could earn S$1,000 a month as a construction worker, but I had to pay S$9,000 to the training centre and another S$9,000 in agent fees before I could arrive. My family had to sell land, borrow money and even take out a bank loan to pay for it all.

We were contracted to build a social housing development in Sembawang. I was paid the promised S$1,000 a month for the first five months, but didn't get any payment for overtime. Then for three months we got no salary at all. We thought our boss would pay us eventually, but then we discovered he'd fled Singapore. There's no way to get the money from him now.

I have my parents, three sisters and a brother to look after. Now they have to depend on my brother, because I have no money to send home.

All I've done is make problems for them. We weren't able to make the monthly repayments, so now we're in trouble. There's a 20% fine on the loan, and men from the bank go to my parents' house every day, shouting at them to pay it back. If we still can't pay back the bank, they're going to seize the deeds for my family's land. The bank's also lodged a police report against me, so when I do go back to Bangladesh, I might be detained.

We don't have a lawyer, and I don't have any money left to pay the agent. I don't know what I'm going to do when I get back home.

[…]

Mario, 26, Peru: Kept in Conditions of Forced Labour in a Gold Mine in Peru

I was living with my aunt in Cusco when a school friend introduced me to Señor Carlos. He'd worked with him in the gold mines and said he was trustworthy. He said I could make good money fast and the work wasn't that hard, all I needed to bring was my birth certificate. I packed a small bag and left. I was 16.

We went to Puerto Maldonado, then left for La Pampa. To get good land and good gold, you need to try different sites, so that's what we did. We worked from 5 am to midnight and would eat while we worked. My pay was 1,500 soles (£372) a month, but I was new to the job and didn't know where or how to keep my money safe, because miners are always drunk, and keeping money or gold around is dangerous. You can get killed if someone thinks you robbed them. Señor Carlos offered to keep my salary for me, and would give me 100 or 200 soles to buy clothes or shoes for work.

I stayed for a year doing different jobs. At first, we'd get 20 or 30 grams a shift, but then they bought two motors and the shifts changed. I started working 24 hours straight and was getting tired and sick all the time, but they didn't let us take any days off. People were dying inside the mines, and their bodies would just be taken away and dumped outside. No one said anything about it, and nobody asked.

One day, I saw a nice guy I knew from the mine leaving with Señor Carlos. The next day, the guy was dead. I was terrified. I asked Señor Carlos for all my cash at the end of my shift, but he refused, and said he wouldn't give me my documents back, either. Then he beat me up and threatened to kill me. He drove me out to the middle of the jungle and dumped me in between the mine and the highway. Even now, all these years later, I'm terrified he'll find me.

These days I drive a mototaxi. It doesn't pay great, but it lets me rent a room all to myself. If I could choose anything, I'd study to be a veterinarian. I like animals a lot, they're kinder than humans.

Young-soon, 80, North Korea: Former Prisoner and Forced Labourer

I met Seong Hye-rim at a school for North Korean elites. That was where I learned to dance. She was a singer, a very good one. Seong and I stayed friends long into our 30s. One day, she told me she was moving to "Residence Number 5," where the great leader Kim Jong-il's family lived. She looked very happy. I asked what would happen to her existing family, but she didn't answer and I never saw her again.

A few months later, I was given orders by the Communist party to go on a business trip. I left my nine-month-old son with my mother and went to the train station. A lieutenant colonel put me in a jeep and drove us down a pitch-dark road. I had no idea what was happening. That first night in captivity was the longest of my life. I was forced to write down the history of my entire existence, including who I had ever met and what I had ever said. It amounted to 200 pages.

I spent the next two months in solitary confinement. Then they moved me, my parents and my four children to Yodok, an internment camp for political prisoners. We all lived in a cramped thatched hut with a mud floor, and were woken at 3:30 am to work on the corn fields until sunset. The only food we were given was gruel. To survive, we found anything that grew or moved and ate it, quickly, so no one would catch us. On a lucky day, we would find a rat or a snake and share it.

I was in that camp for nine years. My parents and my eight-year-old son died of malnutrition there, and the rest of my family were either shot dead or drowned. Later, after I was released, I was told we'd been imprisoned because I knew about Kim Jong-Il's relationship with Seong.

I managed to escape to South Korea, and the first thing I got here was a potato. I don't know why, but I've kept it all these years in the fridge. When I look at it, I feel happy. I know I can get food here anytime, anywhere.

Nelson, 46, Brazil: Trapped with his Family in Forced Labour on a Coffee Farm

I was born here in Tanhaçu, where it hardly ever rains. The droughts are terrible. There's no water, no food, and no point having land that you can't grow anything on.

Some friends told me there was work on a coffee farm down in Minas Gerais, about 1,200km from here, so we decided to go. I called the farmer and arranged for us all to work on the coffee harvest. There was a group of us: me, my wife Leni, our niece Keila, who lives with us, and a couple of friends. We all travelled down together.

As soon as we got there, we realised we were in trouble. Our "lodgings" were a decrepit house that had been left to rot by the farmer; it was close to collapse and totally unfit for living. There were no beds. No mattresses. No kitchen. No cupboards to store any food in or closets to hang any of our belongings. No toilets. It stank of something rotten, and the air was so humid that we had to line the floor with a black tarpaulin just to keep the moisture off of us as we slept. We had no bedding, so we just slept on the floor like that.

The work was exhausting: 11 hours a day, seven days a week, without even a drop of water to drink—there was no drinking water on the farm. We became hostages, with no food or payment for any of the harvesting we were doing. The owner just bullied and humiliated us.

Three months went by like this. Then, one day, when I went into the city to find food, I called a local union for help. They complained to the ministry of labour, which eventually rescued us from that hell.

Today we're back on our own land, relieved that those moments of terror are behind us. Water is still scarce. Even though I dug a well, the little trickle that comes out isn't drinkable. A municipal truck delivers drinking water once a month, so we have to rely on that.

While we wait for rain, I tend the watermelon plantation that I started, and Leni likes to look after the small garden beside the house. Life is still precarious, but we are back home and we are free.

In Nigeria, an Alarming Number of Underage Girls Are Being Trafficked into Sexual Slavery

Claudia Torrisi

In the following viewpoint Claudia Torrisi traces the trafficking of underage Nigerian girls from their abduction in Africa to their arrival in her city, Catania, a port on the Ionian Sea and the second largest city in Sicily, Italy. The author emphasizes the the extent to which these girls are willing to provide details about the trafficking chain. Claudia Torrisi is an Italian freelance journalist who focuses on social issues such as migration and civil rights. She contributes to Valigia Blu, VICE Italia, Open Migration, *and writes a monthly column for* openDemocracy.net, *which deals with women's rights and gender issues.*

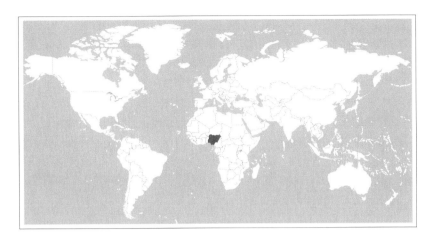

As you read, consider the following questions:

1. According to this viewpoint, voodoo plays a large role in the abuse of the young trafficking victims. How is this unique to a culture, and what do you think are similar methods of control in Western cultures?

2. What do you think is the general tone of the author writing about these girls? How would you describe it?

3. In context with what you surmise from the other articles in this book, what do you think might be increasing the number of underage victims originating in Nigeria?

From the late afternoon on, the pavements around Catania's railway station start filling with young girls waiting for their customers. Lucia Genovese, who works for the street unit of the Penelope association, has been meeting them for years to offer her help and support. "Together with my fellow workers, we move around the main roads or the city centre, depending on where they station themselves. Each place has its own peculiarities, but Nigerian girls are everywhere," she says. Their presence seems to have strongly increased in the last months: "Previously we managed to cover the entire city with one street unit [one of the ways to approach trafficking victims], but now it's impossible. We were forced to split it up into areas."

In fact, the "sex trafficking" phenomenon is experiencing exponential growth. According to the latest report of the International Organization for Migration (IOM), the number of potential human trafficking victims arriving in Italy by sea has increased by more than 600 per cent over the last three years, soaring from 1,500 in 2014 to more than 11,000 in 2016. In Italy, almost all of them are Nigerian women. This growing trend has continued for the first six months of 2017 too.

The victims are very young girls, mostly under-age, coming from different regions of Nigeria: Edo, Delta, Lagos, Ogun, Anambra, Imo. In 2016, the country ranked first in terms of the number of arrivals on the Italian coasts, with a particular increase in women and unaccompanied minors. IOM maintains that about 80 per cent of those Nigerian female migrants who arrived by sea in 2016 ended up being exploited as sexual slaves.

"Sex trafficking is an extremely complex phenomenon that proves very difficult to fight. In Italy we are only able to see a part of it, from the arrival on our coasts onwards," explains Lina Trovato, the public prosecutor trying to counter trafficking from one of the most active prosecutor's offices in all of Italy: Catania. As many as 31 legal proceedings were instituted here in 2016—almost half of the overall 71 that were filed in Italy. Between January and June 2017, there were already 26 legal actions, and they seem bound to exceed last year's figure.

Nigeria, Where Trafficking Begins

The first stage of the process is "recruiting": the girl is approached by a friend, relative, or someone she trusts who offers to help her reach Europe and put her in touch with other people. "This proposal aims to lure girls in extremely poor living conditions. Sometimes they are perfectly aware of what awaits them, but they consider it a better perspective," Trovato says. In larger families, it is often the elder daughters who undertake this journey to help their relatives. Unfortunately, most of the time, the victim has no idea of what will happen: somebody tricks her by talking about a friend who is looking for a shop assistant, hair-plaiter, or babysitter in Italy.

According to IOM's report, "the ever earlier age of Nigerian girls arriving by sea is inversely proportional to their awareness of sex trafficking and of the violence and abuse" they will face. Several teenagers confided to the operators that "they have never had sexual intercourse and are completely unaware of contraceptive methods or the risk of contracting sexually transmitted diseases," and that they seem to have no idea of "what prostitution means."

The second step is the voodoo ritual where a Juju spell is cast: the girls must agree to pay back those who bring them to Italy (usually between 25 and 30,000 euros) without escaping, calling the police, or naming their traffickers. The main threat in case of disobedience is death, either for them or for their relatives.

This spell is one of the elements that ties thousands of women to sexual slavery. According to IOM, voodoo is a widespread "psychological control method" in Nigeria, where it represents a "warranty of loyalty and, above all, silence, even when the migrant discovers what her real condition is going to be." In a reportage published by Thomson Reuters Foundation a shaman in the village of Amedokhian, in southern Nigeria, explains how he scares the girls after making them drink "concoctions brewed with pieces of their own fingernails, pubic hair, underwear, or drops of blood": "I can make sure she [the girl] never sleeps well or has peace of mind until she pays what she owes [...] Something in her head will keep telling her: 'Go and pay!'"

From Nigeria to Italy through Libya

Once the voodoo spell has been cast, their commitment is solemn and the debt to the *madam*—a sort of brothel keeper—becomes a contract. The first part of the journey, from Nigeria to Libya, begins across Niger.

The FLDS Church and Forced Marriage

A woman sobbed in court in Utah on Tuesday as she described how she had been forced into marriage at the age of 14 by the leader of a notorious polygamist sect.

In the most high profile legal action against polygamists since the national guard raided the community in 1953, Warren Jeffs, of the Fundamentalist Church of Jesus Christ of Latter-Day Saints, was brought before the court in St George to hear the evidence against him.

Mr Jeffs, who is revered as a prophet, is charged with assisting the statutory rape of the girl by arranging her marriage. His accuser, referred to as Jane Doe IV, spent four hours describing her three-year marriage to her first cousin. She said that when she was told she was to be married she protested that she was too young, but Mr Jeffs said it was God's calling. "The prophet has revealed this is your mission and duty and what you need to do," he allegedly told her.

The wedding ceremony was a hurried affair in a motel in Nevada with other couples also getting married. Jane Doe, now 20, said she told another girl that she could not go through with the ceremony, and the girl replied: "I cannot believe you are defying the prophet and God's will."

When the time came to give her consent to the union, she could not speak and Mr Jeffs glared at her. "He was drilling a hole in me with his eyes. The silence became unbearable. I finally said: 'OK, I do.'"

After the ceremony, she said, Mr Jeffs encouraged them to "go forward, multiply and replenish the Earth with good priesthood children." On the wedding night she locked herself in the bathroom, but a few weeks later her husband said it was time for them "to do our responsibility" and raped her, she alleged.

Mr Jeffs is the spiritual head of a 10,000-strong community of polygamists in Hildale, on the border of southern Utah and Arizona. He was arrested in Las Vegas in August, having been on the run and on the FBI's most wanted list for 15 months.

His sect is the product of a rift within the Mormon church, which occurred in the 1890s when the mainstream church abandoned polygamy under pressure from the federal government. The Mormons reject any connection to the polygamists who they say are not Mormons at all.

"Leader of Polygamist Sect Forced Girl into Marriage at 14, Court Hears," by Ed Pilkington, Guardian News and Media Limited. November 23, 2006.

The request for this journey comes from Italy or from groups operating between Nigeria and Italy. The roles of the chain are very specific: an on-site recruiter, a person in charge of the voodoo ritual, the madams, and those who take care of the girls in Italy, plus some intermediaries along the way. If the person escorting the girls is "almost at the same level as the one organising the journey (the so-called *connection man*), he is called a *boga*," Trovato explains. If he is just appointed by the recruiter, he's a *trolley-man*. Then, once in Italy, there is a *ticket-man* who, according to the *madam's* instructions, picks up the girl from the centre she finds herself in, pays for her ticket, and puts her on a bus bound for her final destination, usually in the north.

The report entitled "Young Invisible Enslaved" by Save the Children reveals that over the 715 kilometres from Kano (Nigeria) to Agadez (Niger), young victims "suffer violence and forms of coercion at the hands of the smugglers or the many other people who are in some way involved in organising irregular migration (for example, corrupt border police or criminal gangs)." Then they leave Agadez for the border, crossing 3,500 kilometres of desert "in pickup trucks overloaded with people."

After Niger, the girls arrive in Libya, where violence and physical abuse seem to be the rule. "They are lodged in a *ghetto*, *safe house*, or *connection house*. Their fate depends to a large extent on the wealth of those who asked for them: if they are rich, the girls will receive food without being forced to prostitute themselves," Trovato says. But most of the time economic conditions are not so good and, generally speaking, migrants tend to stay in Libya for a longer time with a consequent increase in costs. Sometimes the *madams* run out of money and the *connection men* decide to sell the girls to other smugglers.

Furthermore, according to IOM the cases of sexual assault involving people not directly connected to the trafficking network have increased over the last year because of ever-growing instability; as a consequence, more and more women are already pregnant when they arrive in Italy. Sometimes, when a *madam* discovers that the girl is with child, she decides to "abandon" her in Libya in the hands of local pimps who will force her to have an abortion and work in their brothels.

The Arrival in Italy

Irene Paola Martino, a midwife working on one of MSF's ships in the Strait of Sicily, reports that "in every boat that reaches our ports there is always a large group of Nigerian girls, many of whom are under age … When you separate them from the other migrants, little by little they open up and disclose their unbelievably violent stories." But "as soon as they disembark, most of them change their attitude instantaneously: they keep their eyes lowered and stop answering questions."

These girls usually arrive in Italy with telephone numbers written on slips of paper, which they carefully wrap in plastic to protect them from sea-water and then hide. They always try to follow the directions they were given by the people who escorted them in their journey.

According to Trovato, "smugglers know the Italian system perfectly. For this reason, they instruct the girls to pretend they are of age—because that way they'll be more free—and to tell a certain story. Apparently, Libya is full of 'benefactors' who help young girls leave."

Most of the time victims pretend that the smugglers are their uncles, husbands, or brothers so as not to be separated from them. But, as IOM clarifies, they are actually the *bogas*, "who will hand them over to the smuggler waiting for them in Europe. In criminal networks, they are nothing but carriers who deliver 'goods.'"

This is why effective identification upon arrival is fundamental. In its latest report, the GRETA (European Group of Experts on Action against Trafficking in Human Beings) highlighted that Italian authorities carry out this procedure too hurriedly to notice any trafficking victims.

A Difficult Investigation

When Trovato began to deal with trafficking she was struck by the huge difference in numbers between IOM's reported cases and legal proceedings in the prosecutor's office of Catania: "I wondered how it was possible that the Organisation for Migration reported so many trafficking victims while we only had two or three dossiers," she recalls. Then she started tracing the girls' stories backwards, sifting through the lists of disembarked boats and vulnerable cases signalled to the juvenile court.

Only a handful of them had been reported to the police. Approximately 11,000 girls from Nigeria arrived in Sicily, Apulia, and Calabria in 2016: according to IOM's indicators, 8,277 were potential trafficking victims, 6,599 of whom were identified as such with some reasonable certainty. Despite these numbers—already lower than reality—only 78 cases were denounced.

In the opinion of Oriana Cannavò, head of Catania's section of the Penelope association, "fear often prevails. The choice is far from simple; it is about giving up a certain kind of life the girls were expecting, a migration project that turned out to be a fraud."

Another important aspect concerns the spell and the threats to the girls' relatives in Nigeria: when the girls refuse to reach the *madams* as soon as they can, local criminals scare their parents who in turn immediately go after their daughters. Many of them yield to the pressure and, though they had started to cooperate with the police, go back to their exploiters.

Since it is impossible to rely on victims' testimonies, investigations usually begin when the juvenile court or prosecutor, a guardian, or a reception centre operator reports a particular case. "For example, twice we started from a centre where a suitcase with a mobile phone and a pair of stilettos was found," Trovato says.

In many cases even the victims' statements are unreliable. "Girls do hate their *madams*, but they are also grateful to them for helping them reach Italy. It is very difficult to obtain their names," the prosecutor explains. Some girls even say their *madams* found them crying on the street and took them in. In these cases, they can be charged with giving false testimony. This is the reason why "we need lawyers who are trafficking experts, so that during their depositions the girls can admit they have lied out of fear."

Investigations also reveal that these kinds of criminals are primarily Nigerian. Furthermore, 80 per cent of those arrested are women. The ugly truth behind this figure is that almost all of them are former victims. "Trafficking is a vicious circle: many girls not only hope to free themselves and pay off their debt, they also want to become *madams* themselves after a few years so they can find another woman to replace them on the street," Trovato reveals. Sometimes they are even encouraged by their parents. "During an investigation we listened to a phone call with a girl's mother who was saying to her daughter: 'Don't give up! Today you are at her service, but in a year's time, if you're lucky, you'll have someone at your service.'"

Escaping Human Traffickers

The street unit is one of the ways to approach trafficking victims. Operators mostly give healthcare support: blood tests, termination of pregnancy, medical examinations. As Lucia Genovese clarifies, "we don't talk about protection programs because on the streets you might run into a *madam*." Non-verbal communication is fundamental in these conversations: "If I ask a girl some questions and she keeps looking at the same person before answering, I try to make up an excuse to have her come to my office. Some of them actually end up opening their hearts." But not everyone decides to talk to the police. "Some want to continue paying because they are too afraid for their family," the operator explains. Others, despite having paid off their debts, keep prostituting themselves or become *madams*.

As provided for by Article 18 of the Consolidated Law on Immigration, those who start a protection program are granted a special residence permit. They are accommodated to specific facilities, some of which have secret addresses, and supported by the association in every aspect concerning contact with police headquarters, deposition (which is always a traumatic moment), school enrolment, and apprenticeship activation. The goal is to make them independent, in spite of the difficulties.

In February 2016, the Italian Council of Ministers adopted the National Plan against Human Trafficking to systematise some courses of action. One of the objections raised by the associations working in this sector is that the funds to counter sex trafficking continue to be connected to single projects without being used at a structural level. As Cannavò highlights, "I would like to see Penelope's activity become systemic and the fight against human trafficking become a constant priority for institutions. This plan was expected, and it certainly represents a turning point. But it's only a drop in the ocean."

Periodical and Internet Sources Bibliography

The following articles have been selected to supplement the diverse views presented in this chapter.

Michael Bos, "Trafficking in Human Organs," European Parliament's Subcommittee on Human Rights, June 19, 2015. https://www.europarl.europa.eu/RegData/etudes/STUD/2015/549055/EXPO_STU%282015%29549055_EN.pdf.

Dave Collins, "Case Reveals Shame, Trauma of Male Sex Trafficking Victims," AP News, November 15, 2018. https://www.apnews.com/a7d41311016c415390477750e369f8f9.

Bobby J. Guidroz, "The Different Types of Human Trafficking," *Daily World*, September 12, 2017. https://www.dailyworld.com/story/news/local/2017/09/12/different-types-human-trafficking/653825001/.

INTERPOL, "Types of Human Trafficking," INTERPOL. https://www.interpol.int/en/Crimes/Human-trafficking/Types-of-human-trafficking.

Maizura Ismail, "ASEAN: Epicentre of human trafficking," *Asean Post*, July 31, 2018. https://theaseanpost.com/article/asean-epicentre-human-trafficking.

Joshua Philipp, "Child Trafficking Through International Adoption Continues Despite Regulations," *Epoch Times*, March 15, 2018. https://www.theepochtimes.com/child-trafficking-through-international-adoption-continues-despite-regulations_2464370.html.

Maged Srour, "Human Trafficking for Organs: Ending Abuse of the Poorest," Inter Press Service New Agency, April 30, 2018. http://www.ipsnews.net/2018/04/human-trafficking-organs-ending-abuse-poorest/.

"What Does Modern Slavery Look Like?," BBC News, May 31, 2016. https://www.bbc.com/news/world-asia-36416751.

GLOBALVIEWPOINTS

CHAPTER 4

Putting a Stop to Human Trafficking

Technological Innovations Are Helping to Aid Human Trafficking Victims

Mary Donovan

In the following viewpoint Mary Donovan introduces readers to ways in which new technologies are being used on the world stage to disrupt criminal human trafficking, aid victims, and help vulnerable populations to avoid being ensnared in human trafficking schemes to begin with. Some websites, such as contratados.com, are peer-to-peer, offering advice to migrants hoping to work in the United States and even soliciting reviews of potential employers. Government and private technological applications are also covered here. Mary Donovan writes about human trafficking issues and is a contributing writer at the National Consumers League, a private, nonprofit agency advocating on behalf of consumers in marketplace and workplace issues.

"Technology in the Fight Against Trafficking: Tracking Criminals and Helping Victims," by Mary Donovan, National Consumers League, January 2017. Reprinted by permission.

As you read, consider the following questions:

1. How specifically can new technologies help in the three stages of human trafficking?
2. What are some preventative uses of new technologies that may aid potential victims?
3. What technology do you think has the most potential for good among those listed here? Which countries' technology do you think will be most successful in helping to disrupt trafficker's aims?

From mobile phones to big data analytics, technology can help in the fight against human trafficking. Access to a phone can enable a victim to call friends, family, or a hotline for help. Data trends enable us to study the patterns of trafficking and to know where to combat it. On the other hand, technology is definitely part of the problem of trafficking, as traffickers are quickly incorporating technology trends and social media in their recruitment of victims. This is why it is crucial to use technology as part of the solution.

While each incident of human trafficking differs in specifics, all have three clear steps: the acquisition step, the transportation step, and the final step of forced labor. Technology can help in each phase.

With access to technology, human trafficking can be avoided in the first place. Technology could directly connect a worker with a safe job, eliminating the need for a middleman, who may exploit the worker. Think of the impact of AirBnB and Uber on the hotel and taxi industries. What if workers could locate honest labor recruiters directly with technology? The supply side of human trafficking would diminish.

The Centro de los Derechos de Migrants launched a website, contratados.com, which allows temporary Mexican workers to share their experiences working in the United States. The website also accepts reviews by text message and telephone. Workers can warn other workers, so labor abuses are not perpetuated and new migrant workers do not unknowingly put themselves in positions to be trafficked.

Technology can be used to increase transparency and to disrupt the market of trafficking through uncovering traffickers' attempts to transport victims. Forensic evidence, photographs, and identification of trafficking routes can help detect traffickers.

For example, DigitalGlobe, a company that provides high-resolution images of the earth, is able to spot slave ships in the seas. Using powerful satellites, seas that have long remained lawless can now be policed. DigitalGlobe also investigates brick kilns in India and fisheries on Lake Volta in Ghana, two major industries where child labor exists.

In this digital age, there is a record of anything that happens online. The rise of mobile money makes transactions and payments easier to track. Bitcoin is a peer-to-peer currency that allows users to transact money directly. It is completely transparent, with records of all exchanges, allowing investigation of suspicious payments. Financial data is important, because it is often where investigators discover the first signs of trafficking.

In the last phase of trafficking—forced labor—technology can lead to a way out. A new report from the USC Annenberg Center on Communication Leadership and Policy, Technology and Labor Trafficking in a Network Society, addressed the role of technology as a strategy for escape. The report describes the story of a woman from the Philippines who was stranded in Malaysia and deceived by traffickers. She was thrown in prison and interrogated, but the Philippine government was able to intervene and help her because she had hidden a phone in her jail cell.

Unfortunately, many migrant workers do not have access to technology and are both geographically and technologically isolated. We need to trace the crime in these situations. The Pentagon's Defense Advanced Research Projects Agency is using Memex, a kind of technology that sees into the hidden corners of the Internet, to fight both sex and labor trafficking. Memex scans job advertisements on the "dark web" that cannot be found or linked together with normal search engines.

Another way to fight trafficking is to increase quantitative data and analysis. Human trafficking thrives in environments without data. Complex supply chains allow forced labor to remain hidden. If we increase data collection and analysis, causes and trends can be examined so support can be mobilized and action can be taken. With increased investigation, data collection, and sharing of that data, we can know about the specifics in which this transnational crime operates. Quantifying data also signifies the importance of a problem. In other words, what can be counted, counts. Numbers can raise awareness and call attention to a hidden crime.

Another way technology can reduce trafficking is to raise consumer awareness. The ability to trace goods allows consumers to know if the products they buy are made with forced labor, and let businesses know if there is anything suspicious in their supply chains.

The US Department of Labor released an app called "Sweat and Toil," which shares information about child labor, forced labor, and human trafficking around the world. It allows users to browse countries and products for forced labor, review laws and regulations in these countries, and find out what governments can do to reduce this worldwide problem. There are a number of apps such as GoodGuide allowing conscious consumers to be aware of the environmental and social impacts of their purchases. GoodGuide ranks a wide range of products and gives them health, environmental, and social scores. Red Light Traffic is an app that allows people to anonymously report suspected cases of human trafficking. It also informs people of the "red flags" of human trafficking, so it can be identified and reported.

Partnership for Freedom issued a three-part competitive technology challenge on innovative solutions to end human trafficking. Rethink Supply Chains is the second part.

The submission deadline for the Rethink Supply Chains challenge has passed, but stay tuned as finalists will be announced this month. Submissions focused on the areas of communication, improving transparency of the labor process, and creating tools to map and share information about labor conditions in supply chains. This challenge will hopefully add wonderful new initiatives to the few already mentioned above.

Modern technology can amaze us everyday, with rapid innovation and the creation of things we never imagined could be possible. Like all tools, technology can be and is used for both doing bad and doing good. Using the power of technology in the fight against human trafficking will bring new, exciting, and unprecedented results.

Working with Victims Can Help Combat Human Trafficking

United Nations

In the following viewpoint authors from the United Nations examine the challenges that formerly trafficked people face when they are repatriated, or returned to their prior lives. These difficulties affect all victims in some universal ways. This report uses women returning to the Mekong region as an example, but similar experiences are endemic to most persons returning to other countries around the world. Problems among survivors may include psychological, physical, social, and financial issues. The United Nations advocates inter-agency cooperation in the service of trafficked persons.

As you read, consider the following questions:

1. What kinds of emotional and physical challenges do victims of human trafficking often face when they return to their homes of states of origin?
2. How might individuals from specific cultures adapt? Would returning as a human trafficking victim be more difficult in some cultures?
3. Why might lack of support cause a victim to be trafficked once again?

Returning to their country of origin is often a difficult process for victims of trafficking, in which they face psychological,

Protecting Victims of Child Sexual Trafficking

At the National Center for Missing & Exploited Children® (NCMEC), child sex trafficking is a high-priority issue because children who have been reported missing are often also actively being exploited. One out of every 7 endangered runaways reported to NCMEC in 2013 was likely a victim of child sex trafficking. Additionally, of the missing children who are likely victims of child sex trafficking, 67 percent were in the care of the child welfare system or foster care when they went missing. Criminals who exploit children through sex trafficking frequently target children who have a history of childhood abuse, disconnected families and running away. In many cases, it is this previous abuse or neglect that becomes a contributing factor causing them to run away from home, family, or social services and making them susceptible to the deceptive lures offered by traffickers. Therefore, it becomes the responsibility of every community to establish a better safety net for children that allows for the integration of systems designed to protect children, especially those involved in state care such as child welfare and juvenile justice.

NCMEC is the national clearinghouse for both missing and sexually exploited children which provides NCMEC with the unique ability to connect information on potential victims and offenders in multiple

family-related, health, legal and financial problems and problems in reintegrating into their families and communities. Reintegration assistance, with a view to empowering victims in their State of origin, should be an integral part of voluntary return programmes. It can help address the root causes of trafficking and avoid potential retrafficking of victims after their return.

The *Training Manual for Combating Trafficking in Women and Children*, developed as part of the United Nations inter-agency project on trafficking in women and children in the sub-Mekong region, enumerates some of the difficulties faced by victims of trafficking at the time of their return. These challenges were determined in the context of the Greater Mekong subregion, but similar challenges will be faced by trafficked persons returning to other regions of the world.

states or locations. NCMEC does this by leveraging the information available in our internal missing child cases and CyberTipline® reports. Since traffickers can be transient, this link analysis resource can be helpful in connecting information that can lead to victim recovery and provide information relating to offender prosecution. In an effort to provide law enforcement and searching families and guardians with the most comprehensive support possible, NCMEC has established specialized child sex trafficking case management and analytical teams.

However, the first step in finding a missing child is making sure that child is reported missing—first to law enforcement and then to NCMEC. Federal law defines a "missing child" as "any individual less than 18 years of age whose whereabouts are unknown to such individual's legal custodian." Regardless of the reason why a child goes missing, federal law prohibits law enforcement agencies from establishing or maintaining a waiting period before accepting a missing child report. NCMEC operates a 24/7 Call Center where law enforcement, parents or legal guardians can make a report by calling our national toll-free hotline, 1-800-THE-LOST® (1-800-843-5678)

"Building Safety Nets for Survivors of Child Sex Trafficking,"
by MelissaSnow, humantraffickingsearch, 2014.

- Trafficked persons often no longer have (or never had) personal documents such as a passport or national identity card and usually need help to travel back safely.

- The trafficked person may feel ashamed to return home without having earned a lot of money to support the family or to pay off debts, since that was the reason for going away in the first place. They may feel unsuccessful, as if they have failed their families in this way. The family may also have such feelings towards the returnee. In some societies, social acceptance of the person returning to the community may be dependent on whether they were able to send money back while they were away. Even though communities often look down on women who were sex workers, they are likely to be accepted back—at least to a certain extent—if they have sent money before or bring money back for their families. However, most trafficked victims do not manage to send money back to their family while at the point of destination, because the wages are not sufficient.

- Opportunities for work in the home community may be very limited, wages are generally lower and some may regard the work as more demanding than the work they did in the place they were trafficked to or were in.

- They may have become used to a different lifestyle elsewhere or abroad, living in cities, wearing different clothes or having more freedom than they had at home. It may be difficult to readjust to the slower pace of life and the isolation in rural areas.

- Women and girls who have worked in the sex industry usually do not share their real experiences with their families and communities, because they feel ashamed. They may also feel alienated from their families owing to the often humiliating experiences they have gone through. At the same time, the community may look down on them, considering them to be spoiled and unfit for marriage and as having a corrupting influence on other young people. Some of them may look for a way out by returning to the sex trade as sex workers or by becoming recruiters themselves.

- The relationship between the woman/child and her (or his) family may have changed owing to the trafficking experience. Returning daughters or sons may feel resentful, thinking that they exist only to support their parents and/or families. Parents and family members may also feel they have less control over their daughters or sons or wives. In the case of married women, their husband may have taken a girlfriend or another wife while they were away, or the woman may have a boyfriend. Either partner may want to break up the marriage because they no longer trust each another—especially if the woman worked as a sex worker or is suspected to have done so.

- Some returnees come back with an illness. Sometimes the illness may be caused by the conditions in which they were working, by alcohol or drug abuse, or by physical or sexual abuse. The illness may be complicated because they usually have no access to good medical treatment while they are in the host State or place.

- Those who return may have emotional or psychological problems, spinal injuries, respiratory problems, tuberculosis, malnutrition, dental problems, sexually transmitted diseases, including HIV/AIDS, injuries from assault and complications from surgery or abortion. Illness places an additional financial burden on the family. If the illness is HIV/AIDS, it can also cause social shame for the affected person and her or his family. Some women/children who are ill may be afraid of being abandoned by their families.

- Returnees may be afraid of the police and other officials, in particular if they have experienced corruption or abuse at their hands during the trafficking. They may also be afraid that they will not be treated well because they left the State or area illegally.

- Fear of some kind of retaliation or persecution by the traffickers is not uncommon, especially for those who were trafficked by people involved in other criminal activities, like the arms or drug trade, and have seen these activities.

- So, trafficked persons who return home may have various problems. If these problems are not solved and the returnees are not supported, it is likely that they will be abused and exploited again, sometimes even trafficked once more. Because every trafficked person's situation is different, organizations providing support for return and reintegration in the home State need to find out exactly what kind of support the returnee may need. The necessary information can be obtained through careful planning, prior to return, by consulting:

· In the destination State, the person who wishes to return and any institution or organization that is helping or taking care of her or him.

· In the State of origin, the family or nearest relatives to whom the returnee will go back.

The Best Way to Fight Human Trafficking Is Preventing It from Happening in the First Place

David Denton and Caroline Vasquez

In the following viewpoint David Denton and Caroline Vasquez interview former senior adviser on human trafficking for the US State Department Laura Lederer about human trafficking from a law enforcement point of view. Although the interview is from 2004 (originally appearing in The Yale Globalist), many questions as well as answers remain the same regarding human trafficking. One additional perspective offered here is that for some criminals, drug trafficking and trafficking in humans can be one and the same. David Denton is assistant US attorney for the Southern District of New York. Caroline Vasquez is an attorney in New York. Laura Lederer is a pioneer in the fight against human trafficking; she is a legal scholar, writer and activist.

As you read, consider the following questions:

1. What special insight may someone from a law enforcement background have into the crime of human trafficking?
2. What are parallels between human trafficking and illegal immigration?
3. What are connections between drug traffickers and those trafficking in persons according to Lederer?

"Trafficking as a Law Enforcement Issue," by David Denton and Caroline Vasquez, US State Department, March 1, 2004. Reprinted by permission.

Q UESTION: Could you briefly describe for me the difference between human trafficking and smuggling as related to illegal immigration?

LEDERER: The US law is clear: In a case of human trafficking there is force, fraud, or coercion, including psychological coercion. The definition of a trafficker is anybody who recruits, transports, buys, sells, or harbors a person for the purposes of forced labor or sex slavery. Usually, the trafficker leads the person to believe that he is applying for a legitimate job, when in fact they cross the border only to become involved with illegal activities.

In a classic case of smuggling, however, there is an agreement between the smuggler and the person he transports. The smuggler agrees to take the person across the border for a specific fee and then once they are across the border there is an exchange of money and they shake hands and part. In that case, both are part of the criminal activity, where as in the case of human trafficking one is a victim and one is a criminal.

QUESTION: Human trafficking rings operate both on an extremely small scale and as part of far more complex criminal syndicates. Could you describe the roots and structure of principal organizations involved in trafficking?

LEDERER: Well, they span a wide spectrum: Everything from your mom-and-pop organization where relatives are selling their children—and this is happening quite a bit in Southeast Asia and South Asia—to very sophisticated criminal cartels in Russia and Eastern Europe. These larger cartels employ front organizations, such as banks, travel agencies, and employment firms. You go in for a real job interview, you fill out forms that look legitimate, you give them your passport, they get you a visa that looks legitimate, and then when you get to the new country you are sold into slavery.

The types of cartels don't sort out in any particular way geographically, either. There are also very sophisticated organized criminal cartels in Asia and South Asia, in addition to the mom-and-pop organizations.

QUESTION: Recently in Mexico, many cartels that have specialized in drug trafficking have begun expanding operations to include the trafficking of persons. In general, do you see cartels engaging in multiple types of trafficking? That is, are the same groups often responsible for the trafficking of drugs, money, arms, humans, etc.?

LEDERER: We have seen cases where the drug traffickers and arms traffickers and human traffickers are one and the same. In fact, one of the first trafficking survivors testified in Congress at hearings for the TVPA (Trafficking Victims Protection Act of 2000) that she was drugged by human traffickers in Nepal. She woke up in India, with drugs taped to her body. The traffickers threatened to turn her in to the police if she didn't stay quiet and cooperate. In the end, they sold the drugs in one market and then sold her to a brothel, where she was trapped until rescued by a US NGO over a year later.

At the very least, if human and narcotics traffickers are not one and the same, the money that runs through these networks definitely is used to re-seed various different criminal ventures. In the past, the State Department and other US agencies traced the trafficking routes—country of origin, country of transit, and destination—but stopped their research at that point.

We now are beginning to trace where the money extorted through human trafficking goes. That money often is laundered in an entirely different fourth or fifth country, and then is used to finance additional criminal activities.

QUESTION: Many countries where human trafficking poses the largest problem lack a well-developed judicial and regulatory infrastructure. How does that affect their ability to effectively combat human trafficking?

LEDERER: There is a fundamental difference between countries that have a functioning criminal justice infrastructure and countries where there isn't really a working justice system. In these latter countries, the police don't know how to investigate or aren't investigating, the prosecutors aren't prosecuting, the judges may be on the take—there is no rule of law. Obviously, that greatly affects the outcome.

A recent case in Macedonia illustrates this problem. In this case, one of the judges was a friend of a brothel owner who was a high level trafficker. The case was effectively investigated and tried, but then thrown out on a technicality. Addressing such problems is extremely difficult because a whole infrastructure must be rebuilt from top to bottom.

QUESTION: China currently has a unique demographic dynamic that includes rapid urbanization and a low ratio of women to men due to the added influence of the one-child policy and sex-selective abortion to traditional preference for male children. To what extent do such population issues contribute to human trafficking in this country?

(China has had a sex-ratio imbalance for thousands of years, with the exception of the 1970s under Mao, largely due to the preference for male children in families. Female infanticide long predates the one-child policy, which has exacerbated the situation.)

LEDERER: China's birth limitation program, designed to reduce population growth, combined with the traditional preference in China for male children, has led to a situation where young men substantially outnumber young marriageable women, especially in rural areas. We're already seeing an increase in the trafficking of young women and female children from Vietnam and Cambodia and other Southeast Asian countries to meet China's need for brides. We also see an increase in trafficking of young females within China itself.

QUESTION: You talked earlier about the need to monitor trafficking at all stages, from origin to arrival to where the money goes afterwards. In terms of enforcement, do you think it is easier to address trafficking through prevention at its origin or through interdiction at arrival?

LEDERER: The best way to fight human trafficking is preventing it from happening in the first place. Nonetheless, interdiction can be a type of prevention. That's what we're trying to do at the Mexico-US border, sometimes before people are put into slavery or slavery-like conditions. Of course, some of the elements of trafficking (fraudulent promise of a legitimate job, for instance) may take place in the country of origin.

Once a person has been successfully trafficked and becomes a victim of the physical abuse, threats, intimidation, multiple rapes, prolonged captivity, beatings, and other violence, the physical, mental, emotional and psychological devastation is almost always comprehensive. Rehabilitating that person and reintegrating her into society is a huge task, and not always successful. Obviously, it is better to prevent the trafficking through educational campaigns, alternative education and economic opportunities, and law enforcement interdictions and other operations.

QUESTION: How is the US State Department promoting prevention?

LEDERER: Many efforts are underway, though with varying success. One of the first campaigns the State Department had was called "Be Safe. Be Strong. Be Free." The program distributed a brochure among Ukraine's at-risk population, including high-school students and young working women. The goal of these efforts is to raise the educational consciousness of at-risk people.

Some countries have also conducted general public awareness campaigns by radio or television. However, in countries where such campaigns have been implemented, people tell me that although they were aware of the dangers of trafficking, they still didn't think it would happen to them, and were willing to take the risk to escape their situations at home. So to a certain extent, I'm not sure how effective these awareness campaigns are.

One victim who testified in the Senate said to me that "Yes, they had these brochures, but I didn't pay any attention to them. If they had actually shown me what was going to happen to me, which was gruesome, then maybe I'd have listened."

QUESTION: So most current efforts focus on educating potential victims as opposed to attacking criminal organizations?

LEDERER: Human trafficking, like drug trafficking, must be fought on three fronts: Supply, demand, distribution. You have to address all three at one time instead of just one or the other.

Preventive campaigns without the interdiction, without the high penalties that make it high risk, will not work. Likewise, it is important to address the demand side: the customers who purchase trafficked humans. There is explosive growth of child prostitution worldwide, often linked to trafficking, and the phenomenon is fueled by Western demand, and the US increasingly is addressing demand.

This administration has made it a priority to expose and prosecute these criminals. In April 2003, President Bush signed The PROTECT Act, which makes it easier for the Department of Justice to prosecute Americans who sexually abuse minors abroad.

QUESTION: For the first time in 2003, the US made non-humanitarian aid contingent on a country's tier placement in the annual Trafficking in Persons Report (TIP Report). Countries rated by the State Department as having made no significant effort to fight trafficking, i.e. Tier 3, faced the potential loss of US military aid, educational and cultural assistance, and support from the World Bank and International Monetary Fund.

Putting a Stop to Human Trafficking

Do you think that this action has effectively encouraged countries to be more proactive in combating human trafficking?

LEDERER: The TIP Report is a very effective diplomatic tool to encourage countries to address human trafficking on their own. We saw last year that sanctions do, indeed, work. The law provides that countries ranked in the TIP Report as Tier 3 have three months to make significant anti-slavery efforts and avoid sanctions. Of the 15 countries that were in Tier 3 in June 2003, 10 made significant efforts to address trafficking and were moved up to Tier 2 by the President in September, thereby avoiding sanctions.

At the same time, it is critical for countries to take action simply because of their own will to end modern-day slavery. Organizations like the International Justice Mission can perform raids and rescues in countries where the law enforcement officials of the country are not effective. But the best possible result, the end goal, is for countries to address their own trafficking problems, to have a national plan of action, to have their own preventive programs and their own law enforcement efforts.

Individual countries know the best way to reach their own people. But that's a very long way ahead of us. And of course the point of the sanctions and the TIP law is to act as a lever. It's the stick. We have carrots too, but the TIP law is the stick to show countries it's in their own best interest to do something about trafficking in persons. Carrots include the programs of the Department of State working with US and international law enforcement agencies as well as international organizations such as INTERPOL or the International Organization for Migration to help vulnerable countries increase their law enforcement, judicial and related capacities to fight human trafficking, people smuggling and related crimes.

The needs for such assistance, of course, far out-strip the amounts the United States and other donors are able to provide. So, as important as training, technical or other assistance are, the real keys are good diplomatic and public relations—making

147

governments and populations more aware of clandestine modern day slavery.

QUESTION: Human trafficking tugs at people's heartstrings and thus tends to get a lot of press. Is human trafficking actually on the rise or does it just appear to be because it has been getting so much coverage?

LEDERER: Human trafficking is hard to quantify because it operates in the shadows. Slaves don't line up and raise their hands to be counted. No one can say if these numbers are way up, down in some regions, or holding at an unacceptable rate. According to US Government estimates, 800,000-900,000 men, women, and children are trafficked across national borders each year. This is horrifying, and it doesn't even count people transported inside their own countries, by some estimates, millions more.

I think it is a new phenomenon in some ways. Drug trafficking and arms trafficking made a lot of money for some people who wanted to be in those markets. But as the penalties increased and the risks became higher, a growing number of criminals began to focus on human trafficking.

This transition occurred mostly during the early '90s as a result of 20 years of growing focus on reducing both weapons and drug trafficking. Networks, routes, and methods originally developed to smuggle illegal goods such as drugs, guns or cash can be adapted to smuggle and traffic human beings, as can the necessary supporting criminal industries such as money laundering and producing fraudulent identity documents.

Crime, like other industries, has a tendency to diversify, globalize, and become more sophisticated. Criminal organizations sometimes also have more money, firepower or organization than do governments, at least in certain places.

People always say, "Prostitution is the oldest profession." I don't agree. I think pimping is the oldest profession. But extensive, sophisticated human trafficking as a widespread criminal industry is a 21st century phenomenon, and it can be likened to the kind of African chattel slavery in the seventeenth, eighteenth centuries.

Currently, we're building a critical mass of people who are just saying no, human slavery is not right, and who are compelled to take action. People and governments are coming to the realization that this is indeed a serious human rights abuse, but it is even more than that. The threat is multi-dimensional. Human trafficking is a threat not only to human rights, but also to public health and public safety. When people are trafficked, we see spikes in the spread of diseases such as tuberculosis and HIV. And the huge money involved in human trafficking fuels the growth of organized crime. When organized crime is strong, governments become weaker as the rule of law is undermined and the justice system breaks down.

The Trafficking Victims Protection Act passed because of support from a broad-based coalition of human rights groups, faith-based groups and women's groups. The trafficking phenomenon is proving difficult to stop, though, because of its transnational nature. Criminals are organized across language, geographic, ethnic, religious, and other barriers. Law enforcement officers are also increasingly networked internationally, in part due to efforts of the US Government, but for legal, political and practical reasons, this effort has lagged behind the more nimble criminals. They can't cross national borders without permission.

In that sense, we really need new structures and new approaches to fight human trafficking, perhaps similar to those we're using against terrorism. But we are learning quickly and working hard to get human trafficking under control, and we are hopeful because of the attention the issue is attracting and because we are successfully rescuing some victims from slavery.

Identifying and Helping Child Sex Trafficking Victims Is a Challenge for Healthcare Providers

V. Jordan Greenbaum

In the following viewpoint V. Jordan Greenbaum provides information and advice to doctors and other healthcare professionals about best practices when encountering young trafficking victims. Physicians are often in a unique frontline position to identify and help the victims of child sexual trafficking. The author sheds light on the lives of these victims as well. V. Jordan Greenbaum is affiliated with the Stephanie V. Blank Center for Safe and Healthy Children, part of Children's Healthcare of Atlanta, Georgia.

As you read, consider the following questions:

1. What are some of the ways in which healthcare providers can identify the victims of child trafficking?
2. What are some of the ways they can seek to help victims once they identify them?
3. What are some of the medical conditions child sexual trafficking victims often suffer from?

Human trafficking violates fundamental human rights of children the world over.[1,2] In a global study by the United

Nations, identified trafficked persons originated from 106 countries. Of over 17,000 victims, 28% were children, with girls outnumbering boys by a factor of 2.5.[2] According to United States federal law,[3,4] sex trafficking involves "The recruitment, harboring, transportation, provision, obtaining, soliciting or patronizing of a person for the purpose of a commercial sex act (any sex act on account of which anything of value is given to or received by any person) using force, fraud, or coercion, OR involving a child less than 18 years of age." This definition is broad relative to many countries, as it does not require transporting a victim, and it does include commercial sexual transactions between a child and another person that do not involve a third party controller (sometimes referred to as "survival sex" when applied to the homeless/runaway population). Thus, child sex trafficking (CST) includes using a minor to produce child sexual exploitation materials ("pornography"), using a child in a sex-oriented business (e.g., exotic dancing/strip club), soliciting a child for commercial sex (in person or online), and having a child perform a sex act with another person(s).

Existing data on sex trafficking victims identified in the US suggest that the vast majority are US citizens or permanent legal residents (84%) and are female (94%).[5] However, cultural biases as well as investigative priorities likely influence the identification of victims. There is evidence that males and transgender youth are frequently involved in sex trafficking and exploitation, although they are likely underrecognized.[6–9]

Intersection of Child Trafficking and Healthcare

Emerging evidence strongly suggests that a high percentage of child victims of sex trafficking in the US seek medical attention, and they do so in a variety of settings. In one study of confirmed and suspected victims of domestic minor sex trafficking, 80% reported seeing a medical provider within the year prior to their identification as victims. Most presented to emergency departments (63%), but a significant proportion (35%) presented to a variety of outpatient clinic settings.[10] Their health needs span both physical and behavioral health domains. CST is associated with sexually transmitted infections (STIs), HIV/AIDS, pregnancy, injuries from physical and sexual assault, post-traumatic stress disorder (PTSD), depression with suicidality, and other behavior problems.[10–16] Adolescent girls in one study had a 47% prevalence of STIs at the time of evaluation and a 32% rate of prior pregnancies.[12] Forty-seven percent of youth in another study reported suicide attempts within the past year and 78% met DSM criteria for PTSD.[11] In addition, some trafficking victims experience both sexual and labor exploitation,[17,18] so they may present with health complications related to either form of trafficking.

However, trafficked children typically do not disclose their victimization.[19] Youth have fewer resources than adults and are thus less able to protect themselves from threats and violence by the trafficker. They lack the life experience and the ability to gain insight into the ways a trafficker may be manipulating them, accepting without question the trafficker's claims that the child is at fault for their predicament or that he/she is worthless and must depend on the trafficker. Their corresponding feelings of guilt, shame, and hopelessness may prevent disclosure to HCPs. Many children have deep unmet needs that are exploited by a trafficker—the need for love, attention, a father figure, etc. A recruitment technique commonly used by traffickers is to develop a fraudulent romantic relationship with a victim, which can lead to very strong bonds, despite the presence of violence and exploitation. Children may be unable to accept the idea that their "boyfriend" is exploiting them and may protect him/her by denying exploitative acts or insisting such acts were "consensual." Immature brain development and limited executive functioning render adolescents prone to risk-taking and seeking immediate gratification, rather than analyzing potential dangers and weighing options.[20] Finally, youth may not disclose their exploitation because health professionals do not ask questions.

Very young children may be victims of sex trafficking, especially in the form of prostitution or production of child sexual abuse materials. They may lack the verbal skills to disclose and the social maturity to understand their exploitation. If they are aware of their victimization and are traumatized by it, their symptoms of stress may be nonspecific and misinterpreted by others (tantrums, anxiety, sleep problems).[21] Thus, caregivers and HCPs may remain unaware of the exploitation.

Challenges for the Healthcare Professional

Recognition of High-Risk Patients

To assist child victims of sex trafficking, HCPs must be able to recognize them in a busy medical setting, in which a disclosure is unlikely. Practitioners face challenges in knowing what questions to ask and potential indicators to observe and in setting aside the time needed to ask those questions in a sensitive, trauma-informed, victim-centered manner. They must keep in mind the possibility that the child's parents may be 1) victims of human trafficking, themselves, 2) the persons trafficking the child, or 3) not the actual parents.

Knowledge of human trafficking is generally lacking among HCPs; in one study, 63% reported that they had never received training on how to identify sex trafficking victims.[22] Knowledge of risk factors for exploitation may allow the HCP to identify at-risk youth while obtaining a medical and social history … Fortunately, there is a recent trend toward educating providers about human trafficking[23,24] and evidence to suggest it may result in increased knowledge and awareness.[25] National medical societies, including the American Academy of Pediatrics, are publishing guidelines on the recognition and response to human trafficking[19] or issuing statements and policies calling for training of HCPs.[26–28] Medical institutions are beginning to develop specific human trafficking protocols to guide professionals through the process of recognition, evaluation, referral, and service provision.[29] Numerous resources are available from private and governmental agencies, many directed to HCPs (National Human Trafficking Resource Center: traffickingresourcecenter.org; US

Department of Health and Human Services, SOAR to Health and Wellness Training: https://www.acf.hhs.gov/otip/training/soar-to-health-and-wellness-training; HEAL Trafficking: https://healtrafficking.org/).

Trauma-Informed Care

Knowledge of common risk factors and possible indicators of child trafficking informs the HCP of appropriate questions to consider, but this knowledge alone is insufficient to adequately identify and assist potential victims. Questions must be asked in a trauma-informed, culturally sensitive, victim-centered manner.[34] This "trauma-informed approach" requires skills not usually taught in health professional programs or practiced in busy healthcare settings. The common assumptions made by HCPs that the patient is telling the truth to the best of their ability, accurately describing their condition, interested in receiving assistance from the provider, and trusting of the medical staff may prove unjustified when interacting with child trafficking victims. The provider needs to build trust, assume a nonjudgmental attitude, convey respect for the patient, ensure a sense of safety, and empower the youth to participate in the evaluation and decisions about referrals and treatment. The HCP needs to understand the impact of trauma on the patient's views of self and others, on their behavior, their attitudes, and even their choice of words when communicating with others.[35,36] It is critical to realize that a patient's guarded manner, belligerence, aggression, or withdrawal may be manifestations of traumatic stress and represent adaptive behaviors the child has developed to survive in their hostile environment. Meeting bellicosity with equanimity rather than sarcasm may be difficult unless the provider is aware of the dynamics and manifestations of trauma.

Increasingly, trauma-informed care is being emphasized in training of HCPs, especially in modules covering human trafficking and intimate partner violence. Numerous resources are available (National Child Traumatic Stress Network: www.

nctsn.org; Children's Healthcare of Atlanta: https://www.choa. org/csecwebinars; Polaris: https://humantraffickinghotline.org/; National Health Collaborative on Violence and Abuse: http:// nhcva.org/2014/04/15/webinar-human-trafficking/; Christian Medical and Dental Associations: https://cmda.org/resources/ publication/human-trafficking-continuing-education). However, there is a need for systematic and widespread dissemination of these resources. The trauma-informed paradigm of patient care needs to be taught early in the career of HCPs, as this will optimize communication with all patients, even if the provider is not aware of their trauma history.

Formal, videotaped forensic interviews of children suspected of being sexually abused or exploited are considered standard of care in many areas of the US,[37] and these interviews are conducted by professionals specifically trained in child development and techniques for gaining information in an objective, legally defensible manner.[38,39] Typically, medical practitioners need to minimize questions about exploitation and ask only basic questions that help determine risk and inform strategies for exam, testing, treatment, and referrals. However, most HCPs lack training on optimal strategies of obtaining accurate information and may be unaware that open-ended questions inviting free narrative (e.g., "tell me everything you remember about …") are preferable to yes/ no questions, leading questions ("How often did he beat you?" when child has not disclosed any violence), or suggestive questions ("You told him to stop, didn't you?").[40] Training in techniques for talking with children and adolescents would be helpful to HCPs and may be incorporated into medical and nursing school curricula.

Time Needed to Build Rapport and Complete the Assessment
Time is arguably one of the greatest barriers to HCP intervention in human trafficking. Creating time to build rapport and establish trust in a busy clinical setting is difficult. However, practitioners always make time for the acutely injured youth who arrives unannounced in the emergency department, for the acute sexual

assault victim, for the actively suicidal child. No matter how busy the setting, time is made for situations in which danger is present and a child's wellbeing is in jeopardy. This commitment by the medical profession needs to extend to children at risk for sex trafficking. These children are in danger, they are at great risk of future harm in the absence of intervention, and they are in need of attention. Just as healthcare professionals make time for emergency surgeries, they need to make time to talk to their at-risk youth.

The responsibility for assessing possible sex trafficking and providing referrals need not always fall to the physician. Having a designated, trauma-trained professional such as a nurse or social worker to interview potential trafficked persons, offer resources, and make necessary reports and referrals may be an efficient way to manage clinic/hospital demands. Alternatively, self-administered patient screens may be introduced to identify high-risk patients so that resources can be directed appropriately. Having patients complete questionnaires in the waiting area or exam room decreases the demand on staff resources, although one must carefully consider the circumstances under which patients may be completing the assessment. Safety and/or confidentiality may be compromised if the patient is accompanied by a trafficker or someone working for the trafficker or if a child is in the company of a parent. It would be very important to ensure that the patient has the opportunity to complete the questionnaire when outside the presence of any accompanying person.

Screening a child for possible commercial sexual exploitation assumes the existence of clinically validated screening tools that are appropriate for busy medical settings. Currently, multiple tools are available or being developed, but clinical validation is lacking in most.[12,41] It will be important to create such tools and determine factors that increase or decrease the likelihood of disclosure. Research is needed to inform us of the best way to assess children of different ages (written versus verbal versus web-based questions, the appropriate time to conduct the assessment during the visit, etc.).

Complexity of Victim Needs

Trafficked children and youth have many unmet needs that extend well beyond physical and emotional health, including shelter, food, immigration and other legal assistance, language classes, education/job skills training, life skills training, and other services.[19,42,43] The complexity of patient circumstances requires a multidisciplinary approach to investigation and service provision. Such an approach is not new and much can be learned from examining the practices in the fields of child maltreatment, immigrant/refugee health, and intimate partner violence. The gold standard for child abuse assessment and intervention involves a multidisciplinary team that includes law enforcement, child protective services, mental health professionals, medical professionals, school personnel, and public health professionals.[44] There is a move to use these same mechanisms for multidisciplinary care for trafficked youth by referring them to child advocacy centers for comprehensive assessment and care.

Most pediatric HCPs have not worked extensively with nonmedical partners and may have little knowledge of what to do or who to call. Detailed protocols for clinic/hospital settings may assist HCPs in responding appropriately and providing critical resources,[29] although clinical validation of such protocols is needed. They may delegate responsibilities to healthcare professionals with relevant experience such as sexual assault nurse examiners/sexual assault response teams (SANEs/SARTs) or hospital social workers, who are trained to interact with outside organizations and agencies. The protocols should maintain an up-to-date listing of community, state, and national resources, including the **National Human Trafficking Resource Center contact information (1-888-3737-888).** Adequate description of safety measures is important, as well, to ensure staff and patients are protected from harm.

Conclusions

Healthcare professionals face a number of challenges in fulfilling their roles of identifying and assisting victims of CST. Many challenges stem from a lack of awareness and training, and efforts are underway to provide critical information and resources to HCPs. Guidelines have been published for providers and numerous curricula designed for those who may encounter trafficking victims. Some of this training is generalizable to pediatric care of all kinds and is best addressed at the level of basic healthcare professional training (e.g., medical and nursing schools). The challenge of allocating the time needed to adequately assess and serve high-risk patients is a major one and may be addressed through hospital/clinic protocols, division of staff responsibilities, patient screening tools, and a commitment to prioritize these patients in a busy healthcare setting. Protocols may also assist HCPs in working with outside agencies and organizations to help provide for the complex needs of trafficked children.

References

1. United Nations Human Rights, Office of the High Commissioner for Human Rights. Convention on the Rights of the Child. Available at: http://wwwohchrorg/EN/ProfessionalInterest/Pages/CRCaspx; Accessed on Oct 29, 2017. 1990.
2. United Nations Office on Drugs and Crime. "Global Report on Trafficking in Persons." United Nations publications, Sales No E16IV6. 2016.
3. United States Government. "Trafficking Victims Protection Act of 2000." Pub L No 106–386 Division A 103(8).
4. United States Government. "Justice for Victims of Trafficking Act of 2015." Available at https://www.congress.gov/114/plaws/publ22/PLAW-114publ22.pdf; Accessed on Nov 1, 2017.
5. Banks, D., and Kyckelhahn, T. "Characteristics of Suspected Human Trafficking Incidents, 2008–2010. 2011"; United States Department of Justice.
6. Dank, M., Yahner, J., Madden, K., Banuelos, I., Yu, L., et al. "Surviving the Streets of New York: Experiences of LGBTQ Youth, YMSM, YWSW Engaged in Survival Sex." Urban Institute. 2015.
7. ECPAT USA. "And Boys Too: An ECPAT-USA Discussion Paper about the Lack of Recognition of the Commercial Sexual Exploitation of Boys in the United States." 2013 Available at https://d1qkyo3pi1c9bxcloudfrontnet/00028B1B-B0DB-4FCD-A991-219527535DAB/1b1293ef-1524-4f2c-b148-91db11379d11pdf; Accessed on Oct 29, 2017.
8. Bigelsen, J., and Vuotto, S. "Homelessness, Survival Sex and Human Trafficking: As Experienced by the Youth of Covenant House New York." 2013. Available at https://humantraffickinghotlineorg/sites/default/files/Homelessness%2C%20Survival%20Sex%2C%20and%20Human%20Trafficking%20-%20Covenant%20House%20NYpdf; Accessed on Oct 29, 2017. 2013.

9. Greene, J.M., Ennett, S.T., Ringwalt, C.L. "Prevalence and Correlates of Survival Sex among Runaway and Homeless Youth." *Am J Public Health*. 1999;89(9):1406–9. pmid:10474560.

10. Goldberg, A. P., Moore, J. L., Houck, C., Kaplan, D. M., and Barron, C. E. "Domestic Minor Sex Trafficking Patients: A Retrospective Analysis of Medical Presentation." *J Pediatr Adolesc Gynecol*. 2016; doi: [Epub ahead of print].

11. Edinburgh, L., Pape-Blabolil, J., Harpin, S.B., and Saewyc, E. "Assessing Exploitation Experiences of Girls and Boys Seen at a Child Advocacy Center." Child Abuse Neglect. 2015; 46:47–59. pmid:25982287.

12. Greenbaum, V. J., Dodd, M., and McCracken, C. "A Short Screening Tool to Identify Victims of Child Sex Trafficking in the Health Care Setting." Pediatr Emerg Care. 2015;23(Epub ahead of print).

13. Varma, S., Gillespie, S., McCracken, C., and Greenbaum, V. J. "Characteristics of Child Commercial Sexual Exploitation and Sex Trafficking Victims Presenting for Medical Care in the United States." Child Abuse Neglect. 2015; 44:98–105. pmid:25896617.

14. Dank, M., Yu, L., and Yahner, J. "Access to Safety: Health Outcomes, Substance Use and Abuse, and Service Provision for LGBTQ Youth, YMSM and YWSW Who Engage in Survival Sex." Urban Institute. 2016.

15. Haley, N., Roy, E., Leclerc, P., Boudreasu, J. F., and Boivin, J. F. "HIV Risk Profile of Male Street Youth Involved in Survival Sex." Sex Transm Infect. 2004; 80:526–30. pmid:15572629.

16. Kiss, L., Yun, K., Pocock, N., and Zimmerman, C. "Exploitation, Violence and Suicide Risk among Child and Adolescent Survivors of Human Trafficking in the Greater Mekong Subregion." JAMA Pediatrics. 2015; pmid:26348864.

17. Baldwin, S., Eisenman, D., Sayles, J., Ryan, G., and Chuang, K. "Identification of Human Trafficking Victims in Health Care Settings." Health Human Rights. 2011;Accessed at http://www.hhrjournal.org/2013/08/20/identification-of-human-trafficking-victims-in-health-care-setting/ on Sept 21, 2013.

18. Oram, S., Abas, M., Bick, D., Boyle, A., French, R., et al. "Human Trafficking and Health: A Survey of Male and Female Survivors in England." AM J Public Health. 2016; 106:1073–8. pmid:27077341.

19. Greenbaum, J., and Crawford-Jakubiak, J., Committee on Child Abuse and Neglect. "Child Sex Trafficking and Commercial Sexual Exploitation: Health Care Needs of Victims." Pediatrics. 2015;135(3):566–74. pmid:25713283.

20. Smith, A. R., Steinberg, L., and Chein, J. "The Role of the Anterior Insula in Adolescent Decision Making." Dev Neurosci. 2014; 36:196–209. pmid:24853135.

21. National Child Traumatic Stress Network. "The 12 Core Concepts: Concepts for Understanding Traumatic Stress Responses in Children and Families." Available at http://www.nctsn.org/resources/audiences/parents-caregivers/what-is-cts/12-core-concepts; accessed on Nov 1, 2017. 210.

22. Beck, M. E., Lineer, M.M., Melzer-Lange, M., et al. "Medical Providers' Understanding of Sex Trafficking and Their Experiences with At-risk Patients." Peds. 2015;135(4): e895.

23. Powell, C., Dickins, K., and Stoklosa, H. Training US health care professionals on human trafficking: where do we go from here? Medical Education Online. 2017;22(1):1267980. pmid:28178913.

24. Ahn, R., Alpert, E.J., Purcell, G., Konstantopoulos, W.M., McGahan, A., et al. "Human Trafficking: Review of Educational Resources for Health Professionals." Am J Prev Med. 2013;44(3):283–9. pmid:23415126.

25. Grace, A.M., Lippert, S., Collins, K., Pineda, N., Tolania, A., et al. "Educating Health Care Professionals on Human Trafficking." Pediatr Emerg Care. 2014;30(12):856–61. pmid:25407038.

26. American Medical Association. "H-65.966: Physicians Response to Victims of Human Trafficking." 2015; Available at https://policysearch.ama-assn.org/policyfinder/detail/H-65.966?uri=%2FAMADoc%2FHOD.xml-0-5095.xml; Accessed on Oct 29, 2017.

27. American Medical Women's Association. "Position Paper on the Sex Trafficking of Women and Girls in the United States." Available at https://wwwamwa-docorg/wp-content/uploads/2013/12/AMWA-Position-Paper-on-Human-Sex-Trafficking_May-20141pdf; Accessed on Oct 29, 2017. 2014.

28. American Public Health Association. "201516: Expanding and Coordinating Human Trafficking-related Public Health Research, Evaluation, Education and Prevention." Available at https://www.apha.org/policies-and-advocacy/public-health-policy-statements/policy-database/2016/01/26/14/28/expanding-and-coordinating-human-trafficking-related-public-health-activities; Accessed on Oct 29, 2017. 2015.

29. Stoklosa, H., Dawson, M., and Williams-Oni, F., EFR. "A Review of US Healthcare Institution Protocols for the Identification and Treatment of Victims of Human Trafficking." J Human Trafficking. 2016; 3:116–24.

34. Zimmerman, C., and Watts, C. "World Health Organization Ethical and Safety Recommendations for Interviewing Rrafficked Women." Health Policy Unit, London School of Hygiene and Tropical Medicine, 2003.

35. Phillips, H., Lyon, E., Fabri, M., and Warshaw, C. "Promising Practices and Model Programs: Trauma-informed Approaches to Working with Survivors of Domestic and Sexual Violence and Other Trauma." National Center on Domestic Violence, Trauma & Mental Health, 2015.

36. Substance Abuse and Mental Health Services Administration. "SAMHSA's Concept of Trauma and Guidance for a Trauma-informed Approach." HHS Publication No. (SMA) 14–4884. Rockville, MD: Substance Abuse and Mental Health Services Administration, 2014.

37. Newlin, C., Steele, L. C., Chamberlin, A., Anderson, J., Kenniston, J., Russell, A., et al. "Child Forensic Onterviewing: Best Practices." OJJDP Juvenile Justice Bulletin. 2015; Available at https://www.ojjdp.gov/pubs/248749.pdf; accessed on Nov 1, 2017.

38. Anderson, J., Ellefson, J., Lashley, J., Miller, A., Olinger, S., et al. "The Cornerhouse Forensic Interview Protocol: RATAC." 2010; available at: https://www.cornerhousemn.org/images/CornerHouse_RATAC_Protocol.pdf. Accessed on 5/29/17.

39. La Rooy, D., Brubacher, S. P., Aromaki-Stratos, A., Cyr, M., Hershkowtiz, I., et al. "The NICHD Protocol: A Review of an Internationally-used Evidence-based Tool for Training Child Forensic Interviewers." J Criminological Research, Policy & Practice. 2016; 2:76–89.

40. Lyon, T. D., Ahern, E. C., and Scurich, N. "Interviewing Children Versus Tossing Coins: Accurately Assessing the Diagnosticity of Children's Disclosure of Abuse." J Child Sexual Abuse. 2012; 21:19–44.

41. Chang, K. S. G., Lee, K., Park, T., Sy, E., and Quach, T. "Using a Clinic-based Screening Tool for Primary Care Providers to Identify Commercially Sexually Exploited Children." J Applied Research on Children: Informing Policy for Children at Risk. 2015;6(1): Article 6.

42. Becker, H. J., and Bechtel, K. "Recognizing Victims of Human Trafficking in the Pediatric Emergency Department." Pediatr Emer Care. 2015; 31:144–50.

43. Clawson, H. J., and Dutch, N. "Addressing the Needs of Human Trafficking: Challenges, Barriers and Promising Practices." United States Department of Health and Human Services. Accessed at: http://aspe.hhs.gov/hsp/07/HumanTrafficking/Needs/ib.shtml June 24, 2012.2008.

44. US Department of Justice, Office of Justice Programs, Office of Juvenile Justice and Delinquency Prevention. "Forming a Multidisciplinary Team to Investigate Child Abuse." 2000.

Periodical and Internet Sources Bibliography

The following articles have been selected to supplement the diverse views presented in this chapter.

Brandon Bouchard, "New Report Identifies Business Sector Intersections to Human Trafficking," Polaris, July 12, 2018. https://polarisproject.org/news/press-releases/new-report-identifies-business-sector-intersections-human-trafficking.

Courtney Desilet, "Stopping Human Trafficking on the Law Enforcement Front Lines," *Homeland Security Today*, February 7, 2019. https://www.hstoday.us/subject-matter-areas/human-trafficking/stopping-human-trafficking-on-the-law-enforcement-front-lines/.

Joseph Darius Jaafari, "How to Stop Human Trafficking, Through the Eyes of a Trucker," *Nation Swell*, July 10, 2018. http://nationswell.com/truck-drivers-stop-human-trafficking/.

Natalie Jesionka, "What's Being Done to Stop Human Trafficking?" The Muse, https://www.themuse.com/advice/whats-being-done-to-stop-human-trafficking.

"More Action Needed to Stop Human Trafficking, Exploitation in Armed Conflict: UNODC Launches Latest Global Report on Trafficking in Persons," United Nations Office on Drugs and Crime, January 7, 2019. https://www.unodc.org/unodc/en/press/releases/2019/January/more-action-needed-to-stop-human-trafficking--exploitation-in-armed-conflict_-unodc-launches-latest-global-report-on-trafficking-in-persons.html.

Operation Underground Railroad, https://ourrescue.org/.

Stop. Trafficking of People, http://www.stophk.org/.

Stopping Traffic: The Movement to End Sex-Trafficking (film). http://stoppingtrafficfilm.com/.

Nitasha Tiku, "How a Sex-Trafficking Law Will Change the Web," March 22, 2018, *Wired*. https://www.wired.com/story/how-a-controversial-new-sex-trafficking-law-will-change-the-web/.

For Further Discussion

Chapter 1

1. What is the difference between legal slavery and institutionalized slavery? How does this distinction relate to today's growing rates of human trafficking?
2. Do you believe that legal, regulated prostitution would eliminate a large swath of human trafficking? Why or why not? Support your answer with examples taken from the viewpoints in this resource.

Chapter 2

1. Women and children are the mostly highly trafficked groups in the world, making up 79 percent of all trafficking victims, according to one source. Give reasons for why you believe women and children are most vulnerable. How does this relate to other human rights issues?
2. A definite parallel relationship exists between source countries, which are usually poor or otherwise have regional instability, and destination countries, which are wealthier countries usually located in the geographical north of the globe. Discuss this symbiotic relationship using examples cited in the viewpoints.

Chapter 3

1. What form of human trafficking do you believe to be the most exploitive or damaging? Why? Support your answer with points from this resource.
2. Human trafficking has been said to be a shadowy crime and is generally unseen in the everyday world. What are some of the signs and symptoms of human trafficking that you are now aware of after reading through the viewpoints in this resource?

Chapter 4

1. Many sources posit that human trafficking is pandemic and is only increasing in volume yearly. Overall, what is being done to combat these crimes today?
2. What are some of the more active organizations that exist today that are involved in researching, analyzing human trafficking, and providing victim services?

Organizations to Contact

The editors have compiled the following list of organizations concerned with the issues debated in this book. The descriptions are derived from materials provided by the organizations. All have publications or information available for interested readers. The list was compiled on the date of publication of the present volume; the information provided here may change. Be aware that many organizations take several weeks or longer to respond to inquiries, so allow as much time as possible.

Anti-Slavery International
Thomas Clarkson House
The Stableyard
Broomgrove Rd.
London
SW9 9TL
United Kingdom
44 (0)20 7501 8920
email: info@antislavery.org
website: www.antislavery.org/

Anti-Slavery International is an international nonprofit, non-governmental organization and lobbying group with offices in the United Kingdom. It was founded in 1839 and is listed as the world's oldest global international human rights organization. It works to fight human slavery and related abuses.

Association of Certified Anti-Money Laundering Specialists (ACAMS)

Brickell City Tower

80 SW 8th St., Suite 2300

Miami, FL 33130

(305) 373-0020

email: info@acams.org

websites: www.ACAMS.org

ACAMS is the largest international membership organization dedicated to advancing the professional knowledge, skills and experience of those dedicated to the detection and prevention of money laundering around the world, and to promote the development and implementation of sound anti-money laundering policies and procedures. The award-winning *ACAMS Today* magazine is designed to provide accurate and authoritative information concerning international money laundering controls and related subjects. In publishing this work, neither the authors nor the association are engaged in rendering legal or other professional services. The services of a competent professional should be sought if such assistance is required. *ACAMS Today* is published four times a year for ACAMS members.

Coalition Against Trafficking in Women (CATW)

PO Box 7160

JAF Station

New York, NY 10116

(212) 643-9895

email: info@catwinternational.org

website: www.catwinternational.org/

CATW is an international non-governmental organization opposing human trafficking, prostitution, and other forms of commercial sex. CATW engages in advocacy, education, victim services, and prevention programs for victims of trafficking and prostitution in Asia, Africa, Latin America, Europe, and North America.

Maiti Nepal
83-Maiti Marg
Pinglasthan, Gaushala
Kathmandu
Nepal
+977-1-4494816
email: info@maitinepal.org
website: https://maitinepal.org/

Maiti Nepal is a not-for-profit organization formed in 1993 in Nepal that works to help the victims of sex trafficking in Nepal. Currently, it operates a rehabilitation home in the city of Kathmandu, as well as transitional and preventative homes in the countryside and academies in Kathmandu to aid young women.

The Polaris Project
PO Box 65323
Washington DC 20035
(202) 790-6300
website: https://polarisproject.org/

A highly influential group among those working to combat Human Trafficking, the Polaris Project takes a comprehensive approach to aid victims and also advocates for stronger laws in the United States. It operates the National Human Trafficking Resource Center hotline, offers support for trafficking victims, and works with survivors to develop long-term solutions in the fight to end human trafficking.

Preda Foundation
PO Box 68
2200 Olongapo City
Philippines
(+63)47 222 4994
email: predainfo@preda.org
website: www.preda.org/

PREDA, or the People's Recovery Empowerment Development Assistance Foundation, is a charitable organization dedicated to protecting Filipinos, mainly women and children from human rights violations and abuses. It was founded in Olongapo City, Philippines in 1974.

Prerana
Khetwadi Municipal School (Dagdishala), Ground Floor
Behind Alankar Theatre, 1st Lane, Khetwadi
Grant Road (East)
Mumbai 400 004
India
+91 22 2387 7637
email: contactprerana@gmail.com

Prerana, founded in 1986, works in the prostitution districts of Mumbai, India, to protect children vulnerable to commercial sexual exploitation and trafficking. The non-governmental organization runs night care centers for at risk children and shelters and a residential training center for girls rescued from the trafficking trade. It is internationally recognized for its contribution to end human trafficking.

Stop the Traffik
1 Kennington Rd.
London
SE1 7QP
United Kingdom
+44(0) 207-921-4258
email: info@stopthetraffik.org
website: www.preda.org/

Stop the Traffik is a global coalition which aims to bring an end to human trafficking worldwide. It works to create awareness and understanding of trafficking in persons, promoting advocacy and fundraising to aid those vulnerable to trafficking and to those who have become victims.

Thorn: Digital Defenders of Children
6806 Lexington Ave.
Los Angeles, CA 90038
(310) 804-5208
email: info@wearethorn.org
website: www.thorn.org/

Thorn (founded as DNA Foundation), is an international human trafficking organization focusing on the sexual exploitation of children. The organization was started by Hollywood actors Demi Moore and Ashton Kutcher in 2012 and was designed to combat internet technology and its role in child pornography and sex trafficking.

Unlikely Heroes
PO Box 518
Grapevine, TX 76099
(818) 255-5441
email: info@unlikelyheroes.com
website: https://unlikelyheroes.com/

Unlikely Heroes was founded in 2011 by Erica Greve and is registered as an American nonprofit organization. It rescues and helps the victims of child sex slavery around the world, operating seven residential facilities offering rehabilitation services in the form of shelter, food, medical care, skills training, and therapy.

Urban Light
USA: (301) 523-0187
Thailand: +66-053-271-179
website: www.urban-light.org/#home

Urban Light is an organization that has been set up to aid young men escape sex trafficking. Founder Alezandra Russel started the organization after a trip to Thailand, where she witnessed the industry firsthand. It offers a number of support services to victims, including food, shelter, and healthcare. The organization's address is not published to protect young men and boys seeking help.

Bibliography of Books

Corban Addison, *A Walk Across the Sun.* New York: SilverOak, 2012.

Kevin Bales, *The Slave Next Door: Human Trafficking and Slavery in America Today.* Oakland: University of California Press, 2009.

David Batstone, *Not for Sale: The Return of the Global Slave Trade—and How We Can Fight It.* San Francisco: HarperOne, 2007.

Nita Belles, *In Our Backyard: Human Trafficking in America and What We Can Do to Stop It.* Ada, MI: Baker Books, 2015.

Austin Choi-Fitzpatrick and Alison Brysk, editors, *From Human Trafficking to Human Rights: Reframing Contemporary Slavery.* Philadelphia: University of Pennsylvania Press, 2012.

Anne T. Gallagher, *The International Law of Human Trafficking.* Cambridge: Cambridge University Press, 2011.

Stephanie Hepburn and Rita J. Simon, *Human Trafficking Around the World: Hidden in Plain Sight.* New York: Columbia University Press, 2013.

Siddharth Kara, *Sex Trafficking: Inside the Business of Modern Slavery.* New York: Columbia University Press, 2008.

Kev Kevin, *Disposable People: New Slavery in the Global Economy.* Oakland: University of California Press, 2004.

Nicholas D. Kristof, *Half the Sky: Turning Oppression into Opportunity for Women Worldwide.* New York: Knopf Publishing Group, 2008.

Rachel Lloyd, *Girls Like Us: Fighting for a World Where Girls Are Not for Sale, An Activist Finds Her Calling and Heals Herself.* New York: Harper, 2011.

Victor Malarek, *The Natashas: Inside the New Global Sex Trade.* New York: Arcade Publishing, 2005.

Somaly Mam, *The Road of Lost Innocence: The True Story of a Cambodian Heroine.* New York: Spiegel & Grau, 2005.

Patricia McCormick, *Sold.* New York: Hyperion Books for Children, 2006.

Cheryl Taylor Page and Bill Piatt, *Human Trafficking.* Durham, NC: North Carolina Academic Press, 2016.

Ryszard Piotrowicz, Conny Rijken, and Baerbel Heide Uhl, editors, *Routledge Handbook of Human Trafficking.* Abingdon-on-Thames, UK: Routledge, 2017.

Louise Shelley, *Human Trafficking: A Global Perspective.* Cambridge: Cambridge University Press, 2010.

Abby Sher, *Breaking Free: True Stories of Girls Who Escaped Modern Slavery.* Hauppauge, NY: Barron's Educational Series, 2014.

E. Benjamin Skinner, *A Crime So Monstrous: Face-to-Face with Modern-Day Slavery.* New York: Simon and Schuster, 2008.

Kaye Stearman, *Human Trafficking.* London, UK: Wayland, 2014.

Daniel Walker, *God in a Brothel: An Undercover Journey into Sex Trafficking and Rescue.* Downers Grove, IL: IVP Books, 2011.

John Winterdyk, Benjamin Perrin, and Philip Reichel, editors, *Human Trafficking: Exploring the International Nature, Concerns, and Complexities.* Boca Raton, FL: CRC Press, 2011.

Index

A

abuse, 37, 89, 119, 121, 149
    child, 38, 45, 136, 146, 152, 155, 157
    labor, 52, 56, 59, 89, 111, 131
    physical, 56, 86, 123, 145
    of power, 25, 86, 100
    sexual, 38, 45, 76, 78, 139, 152
adoption, 14, 15, 105–109
advertising, 76–79, 133
Africa, 35, 39, 54, 81, 85, 89, 118, 149
Allow States and Victims to Fight Online Sex Trafficking Act of 2017 (FOSTA), 75–78
Anti-Slavery International, 84, 89
Australia, 40, 106

B

Backpage.com, 75, 77, 78
Bain, Christina, 97
Bangladesh, 39, 110, 113, 114
Box, Heidi, 69
boys, 25, 32, 41, 44, 151
Brazil, 55–56, 110, 116
Brennan, Denise, 21

C

Cambodia, 41, 144
Canada, 39, 40, 99, 102, 103
Cannavò, Oriana, 125, 127
cartels, 142–143
Central Asia, 54, 56, 81
Chechnya, 54, 56, 57
children, 25, 27, 31, 32, 33, 35–49, 52, 54, 59–60, 70, 72, 76, 78, 85, 89, 90, 91, 106, 107, 108, 109, 136, 139, 142, 144, 148, 150–152, 155, 156, 157, 158, 163
child trafficking, 77, 86, 108, 136–137, 150, 151–158
China, 52, 53, 55, 56, 103, 106, 108, 144
commercial sex, 32, 40, 41, 48, 54, 76, 78, 80, 151, 156
convictions, 32, 53, 112
Craig, Gary, 83

D

Dagestan, 52, 57
debt bondage, 22, 28, 70, 73, 86, 88–89, 92, 110, 113
Declaration of Istanbul, 99, 103
Delmonico, Francis L., 102, 103
Denton, David, 141